Classic Quilts

WITH PRECISE FOUNDATION PIECING

TRICIA LUND & JUDY POLLARD

CREDITS

Editor-in-Chief .... Kerry I. Hoffman
Managing Editor .... Judy Petry
Technical Editor .... Sally Schneider
Copy Editor .... Tina Cook
Proofreader .... Melissa Riesland
Design Director .... Kay Green
Text and Cover Designer .... Joanne Lauterjung
Production Assistant .... Shean Bemis
Illustrator .... Bruce Stout
Photographer .... Brent Kane

Classic Quilts with Precise Foundation Piecing
© 1996 by Tricia Lund and Judy Pollard
That Patchwork Place, Inc., PO Box 118
Bothell, WA 98041-0118 USA

Printed in Hong Kong
01 00 99 98 97 96   6 5 4 3 2

Mission Statement

We are dedicated to providing quality products and services that inspire creativity.
We work together to enrich the lives we touch.

Library of Congress Cataloging-in-Publication Data

Lund, Tricia,
    Classic quilts with precise foundation piecing / Tricia Lund and Judy Pollard.
        p. cm.
    ISBN 1-56477-161-X
    1. Patchwork—Patterns. 2. Quilting. 3. Patchwork quilts.
    I. Pollard, Judy. II Title.
TT835.L84 1996
746.46'041—dc20   96-21436
                                                         CIP

DEDICATION

To Nedra and Gordon Hall, wonderfully supportive parents, great role models, and good friends.

To Frank Pollard, for his unconditional support, countless hours of technical advice and math expertise, and willingness to plan vacations around quilt shows.

ACKNOWLEDGMENTS

We want to give special thanks to the many individuals who have supported us throughout this project:

Mary Hickey, for her continuous encouragement, warm friendship, and gentle nudges;

Nancy J. Martin, for her early and persistent encouragement that Judy should write this book;

Virginia Anderson, who didn't realize what taking a class would lead to;

Joanne Meyers, for developing and teaching her foundation-piecing method;

Members of the Monday Night Bowling League quilt group, who kept Judy up-to-date and inspired;

Members of the Seattle Quilt Troupe, who gave us ongoing support and friendship and willingly served as trial students;

Gretchen Engle, Nedra Hall, Teresa Haskins, Mrs. John Lehman, Amanda Miller, Verba Miller, Hazel Montague, Beverly Payne, and Celesta Schlabach, without whom our quilts would still be quilt tops;

The students in Judy's classes, who came with open minds and creative ideas;

Virginia Anderson, Joan Dawson, Nancy Ewell, Ann Feldman, Nedra and Gordon Hall, Bunnie Johanson, Carol Seeger, Gerry Tillman, and Nancy Tupper, who shared their quilts with us for the gallery;

Liesel Lund, for her love, wonderful artistic advice, and firm belief that her mother would indeed be able to learn more about the computer than how to turn it on;

Luther Lund, who has given more love, partnership, constancy, fun, and encouragement than words could ever describe;

Finally, special note should be taken of the following furry creatures who added to this book in their unique ways. The three yearling kittens: Abigail (Abby), the busy, curious and loving calico; Genevieve (Jenna), her litter mate, the sweet, placid and loving Russian Blue look-alike; and Thackery James (T. J.), their foster brother, the wise, playful, and loving Abyssinian-tabby cross. The beloved, elderly Irish Wolfhound friend, Brea, who shared kitten-coping duties and served as a large, mobile steeplechase hurdle.

Contents

Preface

Several years ago, my family and I spent a week in Sun River, Oregon. We went to a quilt show in Sisters, sponsored by The Stitchin' Post quilt shop, and I took a class in foundation piecing the New York Beauty block taught by Joanne Meyers. I spent most of the class ripping out my mistakes, but later, working at home, I was more successful. The next year, The Stitchin' Post offered a class using the Mariner's Compass design, and we took another quilt-related vacation!

Back home, I took a class in Arlene Stamper's clamshell construction method taught by Roxanne Carter. I had always wanted to make a Pickle Dish quilt, and now I knew how to put all this information together to accomplish my goal.

I started teaching the foundation-piecing techniques and was delighted with my students' work. I have found teaching provides a wonderful collection of student quilts and lots of material for a book. With encouragement from Nancy J. Martin and with Tricia's enthusiasm, here we are.

Judy Pollard

Exactly when Judy and I first met is hazy, but the place is forever stamped in my memory. It was at a swim meet—a chilly, evening competition. The children were running around wrapped in towels and jackets, fending off hypothermia. Parents were huddled on hard bleacher seats, clutching hot drinks. In need of a diversion, I leaned over to the stranger in front of me and complimented her on the lovely sweater she was knitting. She thanked me and explained that she had started it for her husband some time before, when she used to knit a lot. Since she had become so interested in quilting, she hadn't worked on it much and thought she ought to finish it at last. I hardly heard the explanation about the tardy sweater. Another quilter! And such a nice person!

Our friendship has progressed steadily since then. We've shared quilting ideas, problems and solutions, and lots of fabric shopping trips. When Judy began making exquisite quilts using the paper-foundation technique and started teaching it, I was just one of many people who encouraged her to write a book. I'm not sure how I became embroiled in the project, but I've enjoyed the experience.

Tricia Lund

Introduction

Classic Quilts with Precise Foundation Piecing demonstrates how to use foundation piecing to make traditional quilts. We have included seven commonly used shapes that can be difficult to piece because of their small size, curved seams, or bias edges. We have also adapted designs that are typically appliquéd. For example, "Country Roses" on page 47 is a pieced version of the familiar Rose of Sharon appliqué design. "Cleopatra's Fans" on page 25 has the look of an antique appliqué quilt, but only its leaves and circles are appliquéd.

In "Basics of Foundation Piecing" on pages 5–11, we describe in detail how to construct the seven units presented in this book. The gallery on pages 13–20 features our own work, as well as other quilters' interpretations of some of our patterns. The heart of the book contains complete instructions for making fifteen quilts, each made with at least one foundation unit. The foundation patterns and templates are located at the back and on the pullout.

Foundation piecing is a wonderful way to achieve accuracy and precision in your patchwork. We hope it will be a useful addition to your repertoire of quilting techniques.

Basics of Foundation Piecing

Foundation piecing is a method of block or unit construction in which strips or rough-shaped pieces of fabric are sewn in numerical order to a foundation of paper or fabric. We prefer paper foundations for quilts that will be hand quilted, and we used paper exclusively for this book. If you plan to machine quilt your piece, or not quilt it at all, you can use fabric foundations, if you prefer. It is easier to accommodate the extra bulk of a fabric foundation when you machine quilt.

The foundation method has several advantages. Because the paper stabilizes the fabric shapes beautifully, fabrics do not need to be used on the straight-of-grain. Use the fabric slightly off-grain if it is printed crookedly and you prefer the design to be straight, or use the fabric on the true bias if that fits your needs. The most important advantage is that this technique makes it easy to sew even the tiniest pieces with great accuracy. The lines on the foundation provide exact sewing guides, so the finished blocks look as precise as the pattern. This method also makes it just as easy to use many fabrics as it is to use only a few, resulting in wonderfully rich scrap quilts.

Foundation piecing does have disadvantages, though. It requires more fabric than most other methods and involves the extra step of removing the paper after the foundation is complete. We have not, however, found either of these disadvantages to be particularly troublesome. The precision and the ability to use a wide variety of fabrics are well worth the extra effort. We save the small fabric pieces that we trim away for other projects, and removing the paper doesn't take long. The entire paper-removal step for a full-size quilt adds only an hour or two to the construction process.

Copying the Patterns

The patterns for each quilt are located either at the back of this book (pages 72–78) or on the pullout. Each quilt plan indicates the location of the foundation you need to use.

Trace the required pieces onto a sheet of tracing paper. Tracing usually allows you to fit more than one foundation on each page, thus saving paper and money. All the foundations include a ¼"-wide seam allowance around the outside edges of the unit. Leave about ½" between pieces when you trace them so there will still be space between them when they are cut apart. The distortion that can occur in the photocopying process is more noticeable at the outside of the page, so you may prefer to leave 1" or more around the outside margin. After tracing each pattern unit on the tracing paper, find a photocopy machine that does not distort the shapes, then reproduce the number of copies required for the quilt. We have not had any difficulty locating photocopy machines that give good results.

Large patterns, such as the Log Cabin, may not fit on 8½" x 11" paper. You will need to trace each of these foundations on larger sheets of tracing paper.

Sewing the Foundations

Foundation piecing is easy to master if you keep these points in mind.

- The unit you place under the presser foot consists of 3 layers: the paper pattern (with the marked side up) on top and 2 layers of fabric, right sides together, beneath the paper. Sew on the seam lines marked on the paper. Stitch them in consecutive order: the seam between 1 and 2, then the seam between 2 and 3, and so on until the foundation unit is complete.

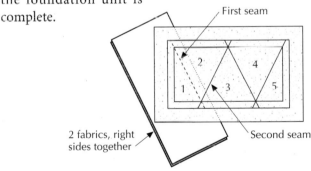

First seam

2 fabrics, right sides together

Second seam

- After you sew a piece and open it, the fabric must cover its allotted place and allow enough extra for the seam allowances on the next seam. The width of the seam allowances is not crucial, *except* at the outside edge of the paper foundation unit. These seams must be exactly ¼" wide so the units can be sewn together accurately. Be sure to allow enough extra fabric around the outside edges for trimming.

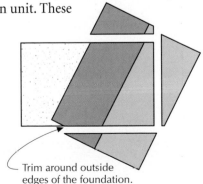

Trim around outside edges of the foundation.

- Cut your fabric into strips or rough-cut shapes. You can use long strips or you can cut them into smaller segments. Rough-cut shapes are quickly cut pieces of fabric that are somewhat larger than they need to be. The extra size can be ½" or more, depending on your comfort level. These pieces are most useful for large, chunky shapes, such as the background of a Mariner's Compass block. The directions for each quilt plan describe how to cut the fabric pieces for the foundation piecing and include templates for rough-cut pieces.

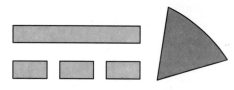

Use strips or roughcut pieces.

- Use a shorter-than-usual stitch length. A very short stitch length makes paper removal easier, but it will probably have you mumbling under your breath if you make a mistake and have to undo the seam. We usually compromise with 13 to 15 stitches per inch. If you do make a mistake and need to redo a seam, you can still use the paper pattern. Just put a piece of tape over the perforated seam on the marked side of the paper.
- We prefer not to remove the paper foundation until just before we sew the units into blocks. This helps prevent the distortion that can be caused by handling. If you don't need to worry about someone handling the blocks, or if you don't have playful kittens, you can remove the paper as soon as the unit is complete.
- Remember, the finished unit is a mirror image of the foundation. This is important if you desire a specific color placement. For example, a red fabric at the left end of a fan foundation will be on the right end when the unit is turned over to its finished side.
- Each quilt plan indicates the number of strips to cut for the entire quilt, but we prefer to cut just enough strips to make one block at a time so we can better plan color distribution.

Constructing the Units

The units in this book fall into the following categories: Flying Geese, Fan, Log Cabin, Mariner's Compass, Teeth, Square within a Square, and Flower Stem. Instructions for constructing each unit follow.

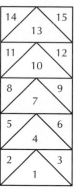

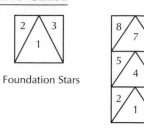

Foundation Stars

Cleopatra's Fans

English Geese

1. With the marked side of the paper up, place the fabric for piece 1 on the unmarked side of the paper. Hold the paper up to a light source to see it better. The right side of the fabric should face away from the paper. Make sure the fabric extends far enough beyond the stitching line to allow a ¼"-wide seam allowance on all sides. Pin the fabric in place from the marked side of the paper.

Fabric #1

2. Place a strip of fabric for piece 2 on fabric 1, right sides together. Be sure enough fabric extends beyond the sewing line to provide an adequate seam allowance. Hold the layers in position and place the unit under the presser foot, paper side up. Sew on the stitching line, through the paper and both layers of fabric. Backstitch at both ends.

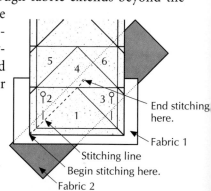

End stitching here.

Fabric 1

Stitching line

Begin stitching here.

Fabric 2

3. Turn the unit over and trim the piece 2 strip at right angles to the sewing line. Trim the excess corner off fabric 1, leaving a ¼"-wide seam allowance.

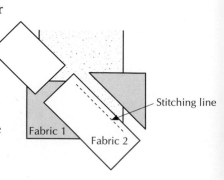

Stitching line

Fabric 1

Fabric 2

4. Open piece 2 and press.

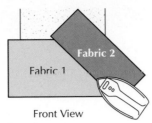

Front View

5. Repeat steps 3 and 4 to add piece 3.
6. Place fabric for piece 4 in position as shown. Sew along the stitching line. Trim the seam allowance to ¼", fold back, and press. Continue piecing in this manner until the unit is complete.

Back View

7. Trim along the outside cutting line. Carefully remove the paper before joining the units to complete the block.

FAN

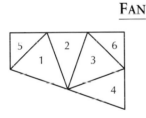

Jenna's Quilt

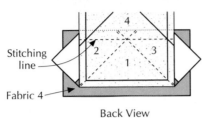

Cleopatra's Fans
Fan Tulips

Heidi's Wedding Quilt

Kaleidoscope of
Spider Webs

1. Place pieces 1 and 2 right sides together. With the marked side of the foundation up, place the fabrics on the unmarked side, placing piece 1 against the paper, beneath position 1. Make sure the pieces extend far enough beyond the sewing line to cover the seam allowances.

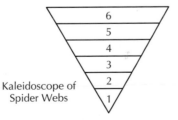

2. Hold the layers in position and place the unit under the presser foot, paper side up. Sew on the line between positions 1 and 2, through the paper and both layers of fabric. Backstitch at both ends.

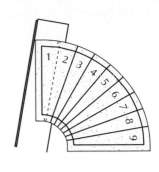

3. Turn the unit over and trim the strips at right angles to the sewing line.

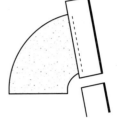

4. Open piece 2 and press.

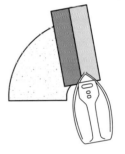

5. Place the fabric for piece 3 on piece 2, right sides together. Make sure the fabric is large enough to cover position 3, including seam allowances.

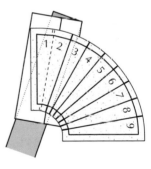

6. Sew along the stitching line between positions 2 and 3, trim the seam allowance to ¼", open, and press. Continue piecing in this manner until the unit is complete.
7. Trim along the outside cutting line. Carefully remove the paper before completing the block.

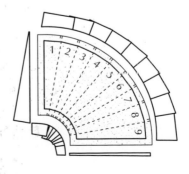

LOG CABIN

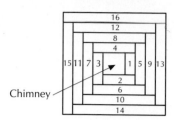

1. With the marked side of the paper up, position a square of chimney fabric on the unmarked side of the paper, wrong side of the fabric against the paper. Hold the unit up to a light to make sure the fabric extends beyond all the sewing lines and provides adequate seam allowances. Pin the fabric in place.

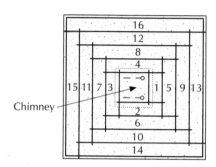

2. Align a strip of log fabric 1 with the chimney fabric, right sides together. Make sure the fabric is large enough to cover position 1, including seam allowances. Pin in place from the paper side. (Fold or roll the paper back to make it easier to manipulate the interior logs.) Sew on the line between the chimney and position 1, through the paper and both layers of fabric. Backstitch at both ends.

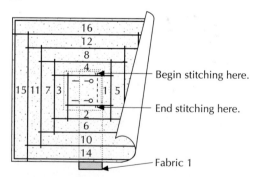

3. Turn the unit over and trim fabric 1 at right angles to the sewing line. Trim the seam allowance to ¼".

Trim fabric 1 even with chimney.

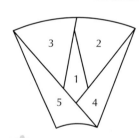

Trim seam allowance to ¼".

4. Open fabric 1 and press.

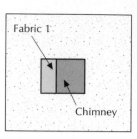

Front View

5. Continue adding logs in the same manner, following the numerical sequence, until the block is complete. Trim along the outside cutting line. Carefully remove the paper.

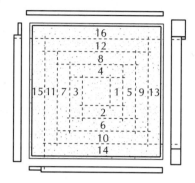

MARINER'S COMPASS

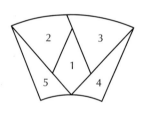

Note: This design can be made with strips, but rough-cut shapes are preferable because they require less fabric and are easier to handle.

1. With the marked side of the paper up, position fabric 1 on the unmarked side of the paper, making sure it extends at least ¼" beyond the sewing lines. Pin it in place from the paper side.

    Make sure the fabric for piece 2 is large enough to cover position 2, including seam allowances, then place piece 2 on piece 1, right sides together.

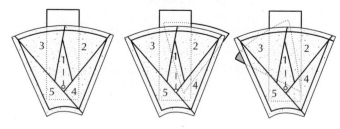

2. Sew the seam between positions 1 and 2, backstitching at each end. Trim the seam allowance to ¼".

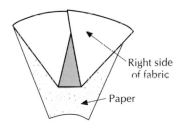

4. Turn the unit over, fold piece 2 back, and press.
5. With the paper side up, place piece 3 on the other side of piece 1, right sides together. Stitch along the seam line between positions 1 and 3, backstitching at both ends. Trim the seam allowance to ¼" and press.

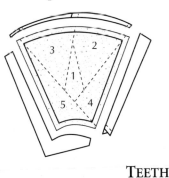

Right side of fabric

Paper

6. Add pieces 4 and 5 in the same manner.
7. Trim the unit along the outside cutting line. Carefully remove the paper along the edges where the unit will be sewn to its neighbor. To stabilize the fabric, leave the rest of the paper on until the unit is sewn into the corner piece.

TEETH

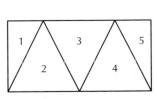

Cleopatra's Fans
Feathered World Without End
Teresa's Wedding Quilt

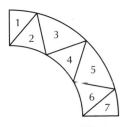

Country Roses
Pickled Cherries
Blue Danube

1. Place fabrics 1 and 2 right sides together. With the marked side of the paper up, place the fabrics beneath position 1 with piece 1 against the paper. Make sure the fabrics are large enough to cover the spaces, including seam allowances.

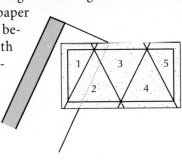

2. Hold the fabrics in position and place the unit under the presser foot, paper side up. Sew along the line between positions 1 and 2, through the paper and both layers of fabric. Backstitch at both ends.

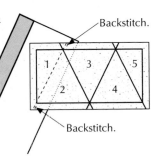

Backstitch.

Backstitch.

3. Trim the fabric strips at right angles to the sewing line. Trim seam allowance to ¼".

4. Fold piece 2 back and press.

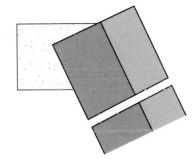

5. Place a strip of fabric for piece 3 right sides together with fabric 2. Make sure the fabric is large enough to cover position 3, including seam allowances.

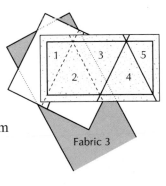

Fabric 3

6. Sew along the stitching line. Trim the seam allowance to ¼", fold back, and press. Continue piecing until the unit is complete.
7. Trim along the outside cutting line. Carefully remove the paper before completing the block.

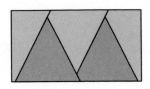

SQUARE WITHIN A SQUARE

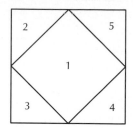

1. With the marked side of the paper up, position piece 1 on the unmarked side of the paper, right side out. Make sure the fabric is large enough to cover the space, including the seam allowances. Pin the fabric in place from the marked side of the paper.

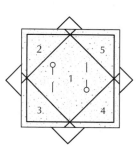

2. Place a strip for position 2 on piece 1, right sides together. Make sure the fabric for position 2 is large enough to cover the space, including seam allowances. Hold the fabrics in position and place the unit under the presser foot, paper side up. Sew along the line between positions 1 and 2, through the paper and both layers of fabric. Backstitch at both ends.

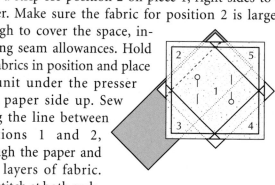

3. Trim the fabric at right angles to the sewing line, then trim the seam allowance to ¼".

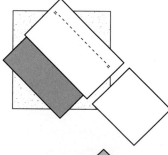

4. Fold piece 2 back and press.

5. Continue piecing in the same manner until the unit is complete.

6. Trim along the outside cutting line. Carefully remove the paper.

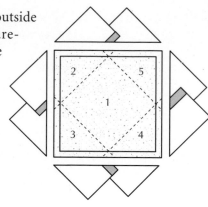

FLOWER STEM

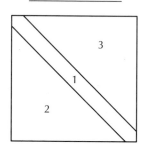

1. Place background fabric 1 and stem fabric 2 right sides together. With the marked side of the paper up, place the strips of fabric beneath position 1, placing the stem fabric against the paper. Make sure that the fabric is large enough to cover the spaces including seam allowances. Stem fabric

Background fabric

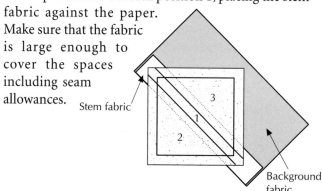

2. Hold the fabrics in position and place the unit under the presser foot, paper side up. Sew along the line, between positions 1 and 2, through the paper and both layers of fabric. Backstitch at both ends.
3. Turn the unit over; trim the seam allowance to ¼".
4. Fold the background back and press.

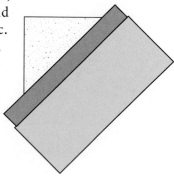

5. Place a strip for piece 3 on piece 1, right sides together. Make sure the fabric is large enough to cover position 3, including seam allowances.

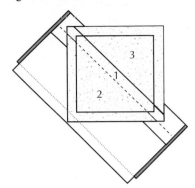

6. Sew along the stitching line between positions 1 and 3. Trim the seam allowance to ¼", open, and press.
7. Trim along the outside cutting line. Carefully remove the paper.

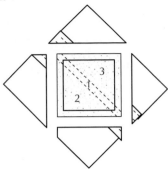

Paper-Patch Appliqué

We have tried many methods of appliqué, and the one that gives us the most accurate results is the paper-patch technique. With this method, you turn under the seam allowances and baste them to a template made from medium-weight paper (like the subscription cards from magazines).

1. Trace the required templates onto paper. Cut them out, cutting the edges of the paper as cleanly and evenly as possible. Take special care with curves. The finished appliqué will be only as good as its pattern.
2. Pin the paper to the wrong side of the fabric and cut it out, leaving about a ¼"-wide seam allowance around the outside edge. (On a large piece, leave a larger seam allowance to allow for shifting.)

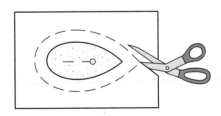

3. Fold the raw edges to the back of the template, pulling the fabric taut. Hold it with your left thumb (right thumb if you are left-handed). Drag the tip of a needle across the fabric from the edge of the pattern toward the edge of the fabric. The tip of the needle will make a scritching sound as it pulls the fabric tight. Baste the raw edges in place through all layers, working from the

back side. Leave the knot of the thread on the right side of the fabric for easy removal later.

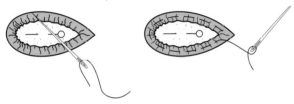

Use the needle to pull fabric taut. Baste in place.

↜ Where the pattern comes to a point of 90° or less, as on the tip of a leaf or the bottom of a heart, fold the tip of the fabric over the paper, then fold the 2 sides toward the center. If there is excess fabric, trim carefully.

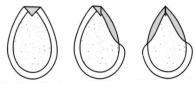

↜ For circles, pin the paper circle on the wrong side of the fabric. Baste a running stitch ⅛" from the outside edge, then pull the thread to gather. Arrange the folds to your liking, then press the edges and remove the paper before appliquéing.

Wrong side of fabric

✎ Make 1 or 2 careful clips in the seam allowances of concave curves. With convex curves, pull the gathers over at right angles to the edge and baste them closely. This will keep the curves smooth.

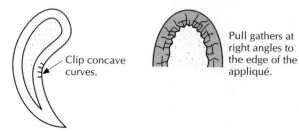

Clip concave curves.

Pull gathers at right angles to the edge of the appliqué.

✎ After basting, press the appliquéd shape. Pin or baste it in place and stitch around it, matching the thread color to the appliqué. Take tiny bites, catching only 1 or 2 threads of the appliqué shape.

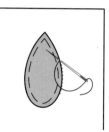

When you have completed stitching most of the appliqué shape, pull out the basting stitches and remove the paper pattern through the unsewn portion. Because cotton retains the ironed crease very well, you can remove the paper at this point with no loss of accuracy. Continue sewing around the shape. Some people like to sew completely around the shape and then remove the paper from the back by cutting the background away. Others believe this makes the block less stable, so they cut away the background only when there are multiple layers of appliqué, to reduce bulk.

HOW WE WORK

When we compared techniques in preparation for writing this section, we discovered that we had slightly different ways of doing things. There are different paths to the same end, as the following examples illustrate.

Judy keeps her ironing board across the room from her sewing machine, so she prefers to sew several foundations at a time, using either strips or rough-cut shapes. For example, she plans six fans, cutting a short strip for each position and numbering the paper fans to correspond with the six combinations of fan fabrics. She chain pieces the first seam on all six fans, carries them to the ironing board, cuts them apart, and presses them. Then she sews the second seam on all six fans, and so on. Judy feels that chain piecing, especially when she uses strips, makes it easier to place the paper pattern just where she wants it.

Tricia, whose ironing board is right beside her sewing machine, likes to have a general idea of what the completed block will look like, but chooses each piece as she goes along. She sews almost exclusively with long strips rather than rough-cut shapes and does not chain piece when making foundation units. When she makes a fan shape, Tricia picks up the first two strips, aligns them right sides together, and places them on the unmarked side of the paper foundation. She holds the foundation up to the light to check placement and sews the seam. Then, she trims the strips, presses the seam, and picks up the next strip, checking it against the light to determine placement, and so on.

Once you are comfortable with the basics of foundation piecing, you will find your own rhythm.

SIGNING YOUR QUILT

One of us has an antique quilt with the name "Ruth" embroidered on the front. While we appreciate knowing even that much about the maker, it would have been better had she given us more information about herself. After completing a quilt, attach a label with at least your name, the place it was made, and the date. Some quiltmakers sign their names or initals on the front, a practice we hope will become more prevalent.

Foundation Stars

Joan Dawson, 1995
Bothell, Washington
23½" x 23½"
Purple stars with yellow centers echo the colors of the lovely 1930s border print.

Wild Goose Chase

Tricia Lund, 1994
Seattle, Washington
21" x 21"
Tiny green geese chase each other among the roses in the border fabric of this lovely miniature quilt. Quilted by Nedra Hall. (Collection of Nedra and Gordon Hall)

Wild Goose Chase

Tricia Lund, 1994
Seattle, Washington
21" x 21"
This miniature quilt was made for a Christmas gift exchange. Quilted by Nancy Ewell. (Collection of Nancy Ewell)

Fan Tulips

Joan Dawson, 1995,
Bothell, Washington
27½" x 27½"
Joan's desire to use her collection of Liberty of London™ prints for the tulips sent us on another great fabric hunt for just the right fabrics for the rest of the quilt.

Softly Summer

Bunnie Johanson, 1995
Seattle, Washington
20" x 35"
The setting for these versatile Tulip blocks lets the owner hang this quilt in several directions.

Sam's Fans

Judy Pollard, 1995
Seattle, Washington
22" x 22"
Judy made Sam's quilt from decorator fabrics used in his room.
(Collection of Carol Simpson and John Gordon)

Compass in the Clouds

Gerry Tillman, 1995
Seattle, Washington
19½" x 19½"
Gerry made this small quilt in a foundation-piecing class. It's a nice setting for a single block.

Mariner's Compass

Joan Dawson,
1994, Bothell,
Washington,
67" x 67"
*Blue and yellow
on a white
background
lend a nautical
feel to this
outstanding
quilt.*

Ben's Compass

Ann Feldman, 1995
Seattle, Washington
83" x 88"
*This quilt grew from one
Compass block made in
class. Ann created this
masterpiece as a gift for
her nephew's graduation.*

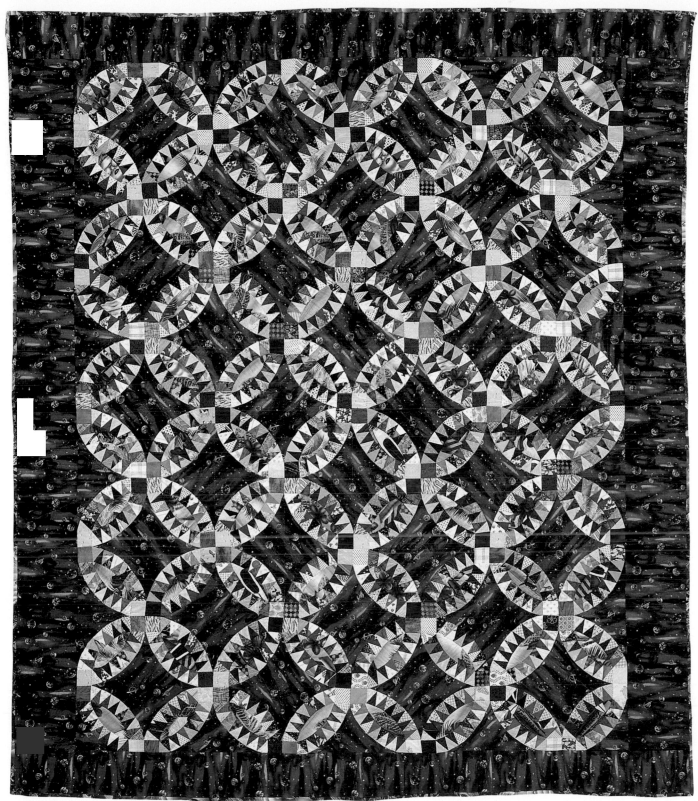

Lucy

Ann Feldman, 1994
Seattle, Washington
83" x 92"
Blue outer-space fabric gives this Pickle Dish pattern added dimension.

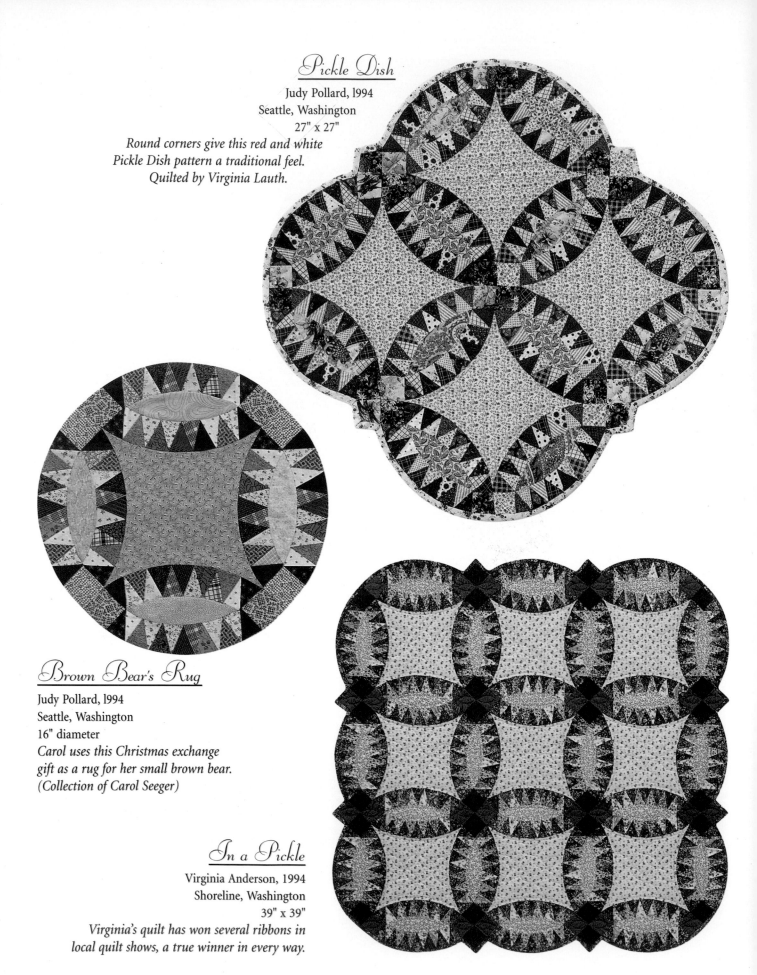

Pickle Dish

Judy Pollard, 1994
Seattle, Washington
27" x 27"

*Round corners give this red and white
Pickle Dish pattern a traditional feel.
Quilted by Virginia Lauth.*

Brown Bear's Rug

Judy Pollard, 1994
Seattle, Washington
16" diameter
*Carol uses this Christmas exchange
gift as a rug for her small brown bear.
(Collection of Carol Seeger)*

In a Pickle

Virginia Anderson, 1994
Shoreline, Washington
39" x 39"

*Virginia's quilt has won several ribbons in
local quilt shows, a true winner in every way.*

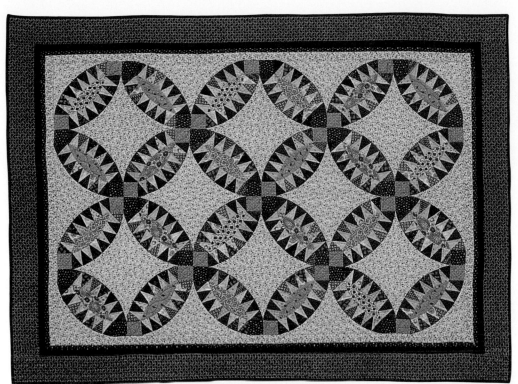

Pickle Dish

Joan Dawson, l994
Bothell, Washington
42" x 42"
Soft reds and pinks give Joan's quilt a romantic feel.

Yellowstone:
Rebirth at Dusk

Nancy Tupper, 1995
Lynden, Washington
47" x 47"
The colors in this Pickle Dish quilt were inspired by a trip to Yellowstone National Park.

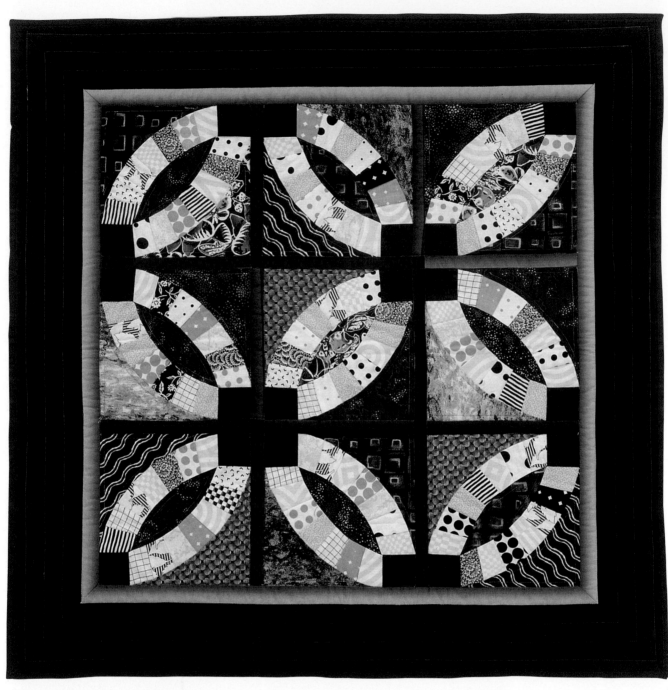

Wedding Ring Variation

Judy Pollard, 1995
Seattle, Washington
43" x 43"
Neatly stacked bolts of fabric at a local quilt
shop begged to be used in this Wedding Ring quilt.

Fan Tulips

Quiltmaker:	Judy Pollard, 1994
	Seattle, Washington
Quilt size:	28¼" x 28¼"
Block size:	5" x 5"

The cheerful combination of blue and pink is a favorite of Judy's, and it gives this quilt an early summer feel. Judy loved the fan unit in "Cleopatra's Fans" on page 25 and liked the way it looked in a smaller size. She adapted the leaves to fit the new block and designed them for easy appliqué placement. The Stepping Stone blocks unify the quilt and hold the design together, as do the repeated colors in the border and prints.

½ yd. light print for background
⅜ yd. total assorted pink, red, and blue prints for fans (For a 2-color fan, use ¼ yd. each of 1 dark and 1 light print.)
¼ yd. green print for leaves and stems
½ yd. blue stripe for side triangles
¼ yd. each of large-scale and small-scale blue floral prints for border triangles
⅛ yd. yellow plaid for flower bases
1 yd. for backing
33" x 33" piece of batting
⅓ yd. for binding

UNIT CONSTRUCTION

1. Make 9 photocopies of the Fan foundation and 9 photocopies of the Flower Stem foundation on page 74.
2. Referring to "Fan" on page 7, construct 9 Fan units. Use the assorted 1"-wide pink, red, and blue print strips. Referring to "Flower Stem" on page 10, construct 9 Stem units. Use the green and light prints.

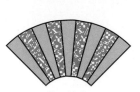

Fan Unit

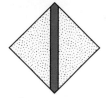

Flower Stem Unit

3. Using the templates on page 74, cut 9 paper foundations each for the 2 leaves and the flower center. Remove the seam allowance from the curved edge of the flower center foundations. Referring to "Paper-Patch Appliqué" on page 11, baste the leaves and flower centers to the foundations.
4. Appliqué the flower center to the concave edge of the fan. Remove the paper from the fan and sew the convex edge of the fan to the curved edge of Template 1 as

---

CUTTING

Use patterns 1–4 on page 74 to make templates. Add ¼"-wide seam allowances to all appliqué pieces.

From the light print, cut:

2 strips, each 3½" x 42"; crosscut 18 rectangles, each 2½" x 3½", for the Tulip block. From the remaining strips, cut 9 Template 1.

2 strips, each 3" x 42"; crosscut 9 squares, each 3" x 3". Cut each square once diagonally for 18 triangles for the Tulip block.  From the remaining strip, cut 2 pieces, each 3" x 15".

From the assorted prints for fans, cut:

a total of 9 strips, each 1" x 42"

From the green print, cut:

1 strip, 1" x 42", for the stem
9 Template 3
9 Template 4

From each of 2 pink and 2 blue prints for fans, cut:

1 strip, 1¾" x 42". From each strip, cut 2 pieces, each 1¾" x 15", for the Stepping Stone blocks.

From the blue stripe, cut:

2 squares, each 8⅜" x 8⅜"; cut each square twice diagonally for 8 side setting triangles 
2 squares, each 4⅜" x 4⅜"; cut each square once diagonally for 4 corner triangles

From the small-scale blue floral, cut:

3 squares, each 8⅜" x 8⅜"; cut each square twice diagonally for 12 triangles
2 squares, each 4⅜" x 4⅜"; cut each square once diagonally for 4 triangles

From the large-scale blue floral, cut:

3 squares, each 8⅜" x 8⅜"; cut each square twice diagonally for 12 triangles
2 squares, each 4⅜" x 4⅜"; cut each square once diagonally for 4 triangles

From the yellow plaid, cut:

9 Template 2

shown below. Press the seam allowance toward the background.

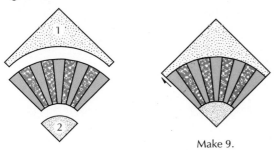

Make 9.

5. Arrange each fan unit with a stem unit and two 2½" x 3½" rectangles of background fabric as shown. Sew them together to make 9 Fan Tulip blocks.

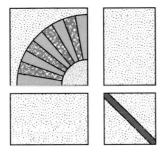

6. Place 2 paper-patched leaves on each block, arranging the left leaf under the right. Baste, then appliqué the leaves in place.

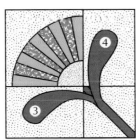

Make 9.

7. Sew a blue 1¾" x 15" strip to the right side of a 3" x 15" background strip. Sew a pink 1¾" x 15" strip to the left side. Press the seam allowances toward the pink and blue strips. From each strip unit, cut 8 segments, each 1¾"-wide.

Make 1.

Cut 8.

8. From the remaining 3" x 15" background strip, cut 8 segments, each 1¾" x 3".

9. Sew the remaining pink and blue strips together, and press the seam toward the blue fabric. Cut the strip unit into 8 segments, each 1¾" wide. Sew pairs of segments together to make 4 four-patch units.

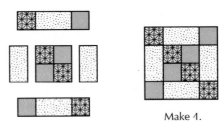

10. Arrange all the units as shown and sew them together to make 4 blocks.

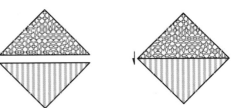

Make 4.

QUILT TOP ASSEMBLY AND FINISHING

1. Sew the large striped triangles to large floral triangles. Make 8 units.

2. Sew the small striped triangles to small floral triangles as shown. Press the seam allowances in the direction of the arrows. Sew these units to large floral triangles.

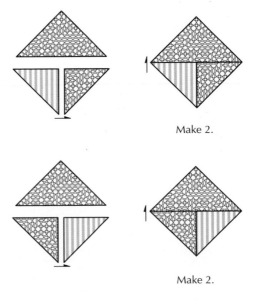

Make 2.

Make 2.

3. Following the illustration below and referring to the photo on page 21, arrange the Fan Tulip blocks, setting squares, and the side, corner, and border triangles in diagonal rows.

4. Sew the blocks together in diagonal rows; press the seam allowances in opposite directions from row to row. Sew the rows together. Add corner triangles last.

5. Mark the quilting design of your choice on the quilt top; see our suggestion below. Layer the quilt top with batting and backing; baste. Quilt on the marked lines. Bind the edges and add a label.

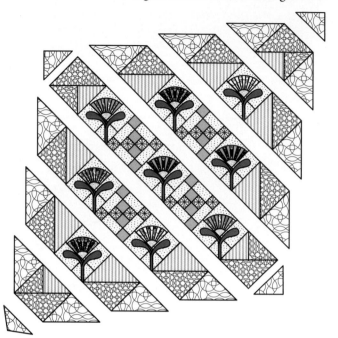

Cleopatra's Fans

Quiltmaker:	Judy Pollard, 1995
	Seattle, Washington
Quilt size:	82" x 82"
Block size:	16" x 16"
Quilted by:	Hazel Montague

Inspired by an old appliqué quilt, Judy tried drafting the pattern from memory and instead created an entirely new block. This is a fine example of the "haphazard" design technique. The combination of green leaves and a variety of pink and red fabrics creates a dramatic quilt.

MATERIALS: *44"-wide fabric*

7 yds. off-white for background and borders
1 yd. total assorted light prints for fans, geese, and border
    teeth
2¾ yds. total assorted pink and red prints for fans, geese,
    and border teeth
2¾ yds. total assorted green prints for leaves, stems, and
    geese
¼ yd. total assorted yellow prints for fan centers and center
    circles
7½ yds. for backing
86" x 86" piece of batting
⅝ yd. for binding

CUTTING

Use patterns 1–5 on pages 72–73 to make templates. Add
¼"-wide seam allowances to all appliqué pieces.

From the lengthwise grain of the off-white fabric, cut:

2 strips, each 2⅞" x 75¾"*
2 strips, each 2⅞" x 80½", for the middle border*

*These borders must fit exactly so the outer border will fit. Do not allow
extra fabric for trimming.*

From the remaining off-white fabric, cut:

8 rectangles, each 6⅛" x 19¾", for the inner border
4 rectangles, each 6⅛" x 14¾", for the inner border
16 squares, each 3⅝" x 3⅝", for the inner border; cut each
    square once diagonally for 32 triangles

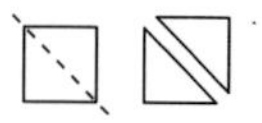

4 rectangles, each 2⅝" x 4½", for the inner-border blocks
4 rectangles, each 2⅝" x 6⅛", for the inner-border blocks
24 rectangles, each 4½" x 16½", for the sashing strips
32 squares, each 3" x 3", for the setting squares; cut each
    square once diagonally for 64 triangles
32 strips, each 2½" x 10", for the outer-border Teeth
    foundations
48 Template 1, for the Fan foundations
36 squares, each 3½" x 3½", for the Stem foundations; cut
    each square once diagonally for 72 triangles
72 rectangles, each 3½" x 4½", for the blocks
36 rectangles, each 2½" x 3", for the blocks

From the light prints, cut:

48 strips, each 1¼" x 16", for the Fan foundations; cut 4
    strips from the same fabric for each block

From the assorted red & pink prints, cut:

a total of 48 strips, each 1¼" x 20" (or the equivalent lengths
    in 4" multiples), for the Fan foundations; cut 4 strips
    from the same fabric for each block
a total of 32 strips, each 2½" x 10", for the outer-border
    Teeth foundations
4 red squares, each 1½" x 1½", for the outer-border corners
108 rectangles, each 2" x 3", for the Flying Geese
    foundations; cut 12 from the same fabric for each block
9 squares, each 2½" x 2½", for the block centers
16 squares, each 4" x 4", for the Square Within a Square
    cornerstone foundations
40 Template 4; cut 4 from the same fabric for each block.
    Reserve 4 for the inner-border appliqué.

From the assorted green prints, cut:

36 rectangles, each ⅞" x 4½", for the stem foundations
36 Template 3 and 36 Template 3 reversed, for the leaves; cut
    4 Template 3 and 4 Template 3 reversed from the same
    fabric for each block
16 Template 3 and 16 Template 3 reversed, for the inner-
    border leaves. Cut all the leaves from the same green.
    Trim 8 leaves and 8 reversed leaves on the pattern
    trimming line, for the corners of the quilt.
18 strips, each 1¾" x 36", for the Flying Geese foundations;
    cut 2 strips from the same fabric for each block

From the assorted yellow prints, cut:

48 Template 2 for the Fan foundation centers
25 Template 5 for the blocks and setting squares

Unit Construction

1. Make 48 photocopies of the Fan foundation on page 73, 36 photocopies of the Flower Stem foundation on page 72, and 36 photocopies of the Flying Geese foundation on page 72.

   Cut 48 paper foundations for Template 3 and 48 foundations for Template 3 reversed on page 72. Cut 40 paper foundations for Template 4 on page 72 and 25 for Template 5 on page 73. Cut 48 paper foundations for the Fan center, Template 2. Remove the seam allowance from the curved edge.

2. Referring to "Fan" on page 7, construct 48 Fan units. Use the red, pink, and light prints. Reserve 12 of the Fan units for the inner border.

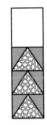

Fan Unit
Make 48.

3. Referring to "Flying Geese" on page 6 and "Flower Stem" on page 10, construct 36 Flying Geese units and 36 Stem units. Add a 2½" x 3" rectangle to the top edge of each Flying Geese unit.

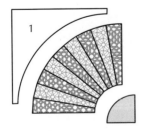

Flying Geese Unit
Make 36.

Flower Stem Unit
Make 36.

4. Refering to "Paper-Patch Appliqué" on page 11, baste the fan centers, then appliqué the convex edge of the center to the concave edge of each Fan unit as shown below. Sew an off-white piece 1 to the convex edge of each Fan unit.

5. Paper-patch 9 yellow circles 5, then center 1 circle on each 2½" red square and appliqué it in place as shown.

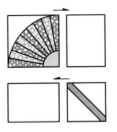

Make 9.

6. Arrange 36 Fan and 36 Stem units with the 3½" x 4½" off-white rectangles; sew the units together as shown.

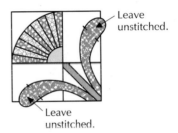
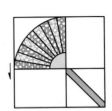

7. Paper-patch the Template 3 and 3 reversed leaves, then appliqué 1 leaf and 1 reversed leaf to each unit as shown. Leave the tip of each leaf free; complete the appliqué after the block is assembled.

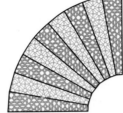

Leave unstitched.

Leave unstitched.

8. Arrange 4 completed Flower units with 4 Flying Geese units, and the red center square as shown. Sew the units into rows, then sew the rows together. Be careful not to catch the leaf in the seam. Complete the leaf appliqué. Add red circles (Piece 4) between each pair of leaves as shown.

Make 9.

QUILT TOP ASSEMBLY AND FINISHING

1. Make 16 photocopies of the Square Within a Square foundation on page 72.
2. Referring to "Square Within a Square" on page 10, construct 16 setting squares. Paper-patch 16 yellow circles (Template 5) and appliqué them to the center of the Square Within a Square unit.

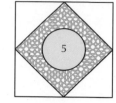

Make 16.

3. Arrange the blocks with the sashing strips and setting squares as shown. Sew into rows, pressing the seams toward the sashing strips. Sew the rows together.

4. Arrange 4 of the reserved Fan units with the 2⅝" x 4½" and 2⅝" x 6⅛" off-white rectangles as shown and sew them together to make 4 corner squares. Press the seam allowances toward the background.

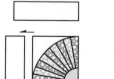

Make 4.

5. Sew a triangle to each side of the 8 remaining Fan blocks.

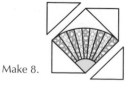

Make 8.

6. Appliqué 2 leaves to each block as shown, leaving one end of each leaf free. Appliqué the 8 short leaves and the 8 reversed short leaves to the bottom corners of four 6⅛" x 19½" off-white strips as shown.

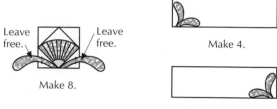

Leave free.   Leave free.

Make 8.   Make 4.

Make 4.

7. Arrange the 6⅛" x 14¼" and 6⅛" x 19½" off-white rectangles with the 4 corner Fan units and 8 side Fan units as shown to make 4 border strips.

Make 2 side borders.

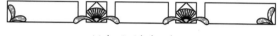

Make 2 top and bottom borders.

8. Add the side borders to opposite side edges of the quilt top, then add the top and bottom borders. Press the seams toward the center. Finish appliquéing the leaves to the border strips. Sew the 2⅞" x 75¾" off-white strips to opposite side edges of the quilt top, then add the 2⅞" x 80½" off-white strips to the top and bottom edges; press the seams toward the center.

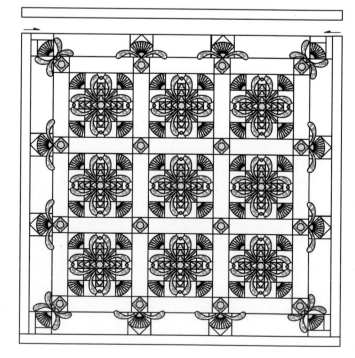

Note: The quilt top must measure 80½" x 80½" so that the outer border will fit; adjust the quilt top if necessary.

9. Make 32 photocopies of the Teeth border foundation on page 73. Referring to "Teeth" on page 9, construct 32 Teeth border units.

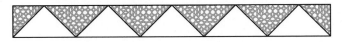

Make 32.

10. Arrange 8 Teeth border units as shown. Make 4 borders. Add a 1½" red square to each end of 2 strips.

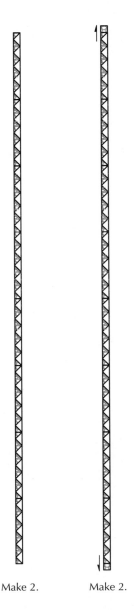

Make 2.   Make 2.

11. Sew the short Teeth borders to opposite side edges; press seams toward the quilt top. Sew the long Teeth borders to the top and bottom edges of the quilt top.

12. Mark the quilting design of your choice on the quilt top. See the suggestion below. Layer the quilt top with batting and backing; baste. Quilt on the marked lines. Bind the edges and add a label.

Kaleidoscope of Spider Webs

Quiltmaker:	Tricia Lund, 1994
	Seattle, Washington
Quilt size:	70½" x 75½"
Block size:	13" x 15"
Quilted by:	Verba Miller

This quilt brings back childhood memories of being fascinated with the colors and patterns in a kaleidoscope. We know as adults that a kaleidoscope contains mirrors and bits of glass and beads, but back then, it was magic that created the shifting designs.

The shading in "Kaleidoscope of Spider Webs" is achieved with a delicious variety of fabrics, from nine to seventeen in each block. To re-create the look of an antique quilt in which the quilter ran out of one fabric and cleverly substituted another, use two or more similar fabrics in a ring. The shading in this design glows when set against a black background.

MATERIALS: 44"-wide fabric

2¾ yds. black print for background and inner and outer borders
⅓ yd. total assorted light and medium blue prints for middle border
5¼ yds. total assorted light, medium, and dark prints in blue, rose, peach, and brown for Spider Web blocks
5⅛ yds. for backing
75" x 80" piece of batting
⅔ yd. for binding

CUTTING

Note: If you cut border strips before constructing the quilt top, cut the strips a little longer than required and trim to fit when you add them to the quilt top. If you cut border strips later, be sure to reserve sufficient fabric length.

Use patterns 1 and 2 on the pullout to make templates.

From the lengthwise grain of the black print, cut:

2 strips, each 1½" x 65½", for the inner borders
2 strips, each 1½" x 62½", for the inner borders
2 strips, each 3½" x 69½", for the outer borders
2 strips, each 3½" x 70½", for the outer borders
34 Template 1 for the background
6 each of Template 2 and 2 reversed for the background

From the assorted light & medium blue prints for the middle border, cut:

1½"-wide strips of varying lengths. Sew them together end to end, then cut 2 strips, each 1½" x 64½", and 2 strips, each 1½" x 67½", for inner borders.

From the assorted prints for the Spider Web block, cut:

a total of 10 strips, each 2" x 42", for the centers
a total of 100 strips, each 1½" x 42", for the rows

UNIT CONSTRUCTION

1. Make 116 photocopies of the Spider Web wedge foundation on the pullout. Number the sections of 58 wedges from 1–6, beginning at the tip of the wedge. Number the sections of the remaining 58 wedges from 1–6, beginning at the base.
2. Referring to "Fan" on page 7, construct 116 Spider Web units. Refer to the photo on page 30 for ideas about color placement. Use 2"-wide strips for the center of each wedge and 1½"-wide strips for the rows.

   For each block, sew 3 wedges from the tip to the base, using dark centers. Sew the remaining 3 wedges from the base to the tip, using light centers. This creates opposing seams on adjoining wedges, making them easy to sew together.

Make 3 wedges for each block.   Make 3 wedges for each block.

3. Trim the units along the outer seam lines and remove the paper.
4. Arrange 6 wedges as shown below, alternating dark and light centers. Sew 3 units together to make half blocks, then sew half blocks together to complete the block. Make 18 blocks. Reserve the remaining units for step 7 on page 32.

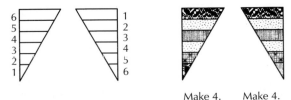

Make 18.

5. Make 4 photocopies of the half-wedge foundation and 4 photocopies of the reversed half-wedge foundation on the pullout. Construct the 4 half-wedges with light centers and the 4 reversed half-wedges with dark centers.

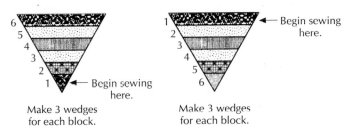

Make 4.   Make 4.

6. Trim each unit along the outer seam lines and remove the paper.

7. Arrange 2 wedge units, 1 half-wedge unit, and 1 half-wedge unit reversed as shown. Sew the units together. Make 4 half-blocks.

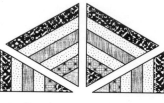

Half-wedge   Half-wedge reversed

QUILT TOP ASSEMBLY AND FINISHING

1. Arrange the blocks and half-blocks with background triangles and sew them together to make rows as shown. Press the seam allowances toward the background triangles.

Rows 1, 3, and 5

Rows 2 and 4

2. Arrange the rows as shown and sew them together.

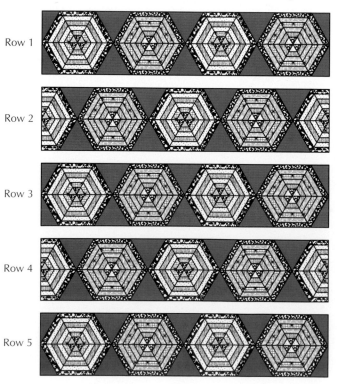

Row 1

Row 2

Row 3

Row 4

Row 5

3. Measure the quilt top for straight-cut borders. Sew the 1½" x 67½" border strips to opposite side edges of the quilt top. Add the 1½" x 64½" border strips to the top and bottom edges. Press all seams toward the border.

4. Add the outer-border strips in the same manner.

5. Mark the top with the quilting design of your choice. See our suggestion below. Layer it with batting and backing; baste. Quilt on the marked lines. Bind the edges and add a label.

Jenna's Quilt

Quiltmaker:	Tricia Lund, 1995
	Seattle, Washington
Quilt size:	68½" x 82½"
Block size:	7" x 7"
Quilted by:	Celesta Schlabach

"*Jenna's Quilt*" is named for Genevieve, the sweet, placid kitten who sat on the quilt at every stage of its development. Her dark gray fur looks lovely against the gray, black, and pink prints chosen to complement the chintz border fabric. Because of its small scale, this chintz was easier to incorporate into the quilt than many chintz fabrics.

The border appears to wrap around the quilt. This illusion is created by the half-blocks that ring the central design. This design is less complicated than it appears, but it is helpful to plan the blocks ahead of time or to arrange them on a design wall as they are finished.

2½ yds. dark floral chintz for border and blocks
4¾ yds. total assorted black and dark gray prints for blocks
2 yds. total assorted pink and light gray prints for blocks
3¾ yds. total assorted light prints for blocks
5¼ yds. for backing
73" x 87" piece of batting
⅔ yd. for binding

CUTTING

Note: If you cut border strips before constructing the quilt top, cut the strips a little longer than required and trim to fit when you add them to the quilt top.

From the chintz & assorted black & dark gray prints, cut:

a total of 23 strips, each 3¼" x 42", for Units A, B, and C
a total of 16 strips, each 2½" x 42", for Units B and C

From the assorted pink & light gray prints, cut:

a total of 16 strips, each 4" x 42", for Unit A
a total of 10 strips, each 2½" x 42", for Units B and C

From the assorted light prints, cut:

a total of 17 strips, each 4" x 42", for Units B and C
a total of 3 strips, each 2½" x 42", for Unit D

From the lengthwise grain of the chintz, cut:

2 strips, each 6½" x 70½", for the side borders
2 strips, each 6½" x 68½", for the top and bottom borders
3 strips, each 3¼" x 42", for the outside B units
14 rectangles, each 4½" x 8", for Unit D

From the remaining chintz, cut:

4 squares, each 4½" x 4½", for the corner units
5 strips, each 2" x 42", for Unit C

BLOCK CONSTRUCTION

Study the color photo on page 33 for color-placement ideas.

1. Use the foundations on pages 75–76. Make 126 photo copies of the Units A and B foundation, 18 photocopies of the Unit C foundation, 14 photocopies of the Unit D foundation, and 4 photocopies of the corner block foundation.

2. Mark color placement on the Unit A and B foundations as shown. Mark on the printed side of the foundations.

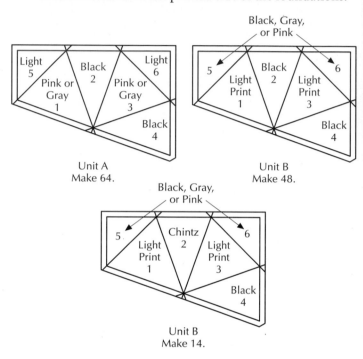

Unit A
Make 64.

Unit B
Make 48.

Unit B
Make 14.

3. Mark the color placement on the C and D unit foundations and the corner block foundations as shown below. Mark on the printed side of the foundations.

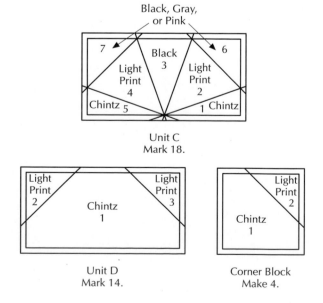

Unit C
Mark 18.

Unit D
Mark 14.

Corner Block
Make 4.

4. Referring to "Fan" on page 7, construct all the marked foundations. Follow the color placement notations and use the strip widths indicated below. Make the Unit A foundations in identical pairs. Staystitch ⅛" from the edge of the C units to stabilize the bias edges.

Strip Width	Foundation	Position
4"	Foundations A & B	1 & 3
	Foundation C	3
3¼"	Foundations A, B & C	2 & 4
2½"	Foundations A & B	5 & 6
	Foundation C	6 & 7
	Foundation D	2 & 3
	Corner block	2
2"	Foundation C	1 & 5

Note: To make stars that have 4 identical points, you must carefully plan the fabric placement in positions 2 and 4 on the Unit B foundations, and in position 3 on the Unit C foundation. Construct the A units first and join them in pairs to make blocks; then arrange the units on a design wall, leaving space for the Unit B blocks between them.

Cut 3¼" x 5" rectangles of the proper fabrics and pin them to the corresponding section of the foundation. Remember, the marked side of the foundation unit is the mirror image of the finished block. Pin the rectangles in position on the un-marked side of the block.

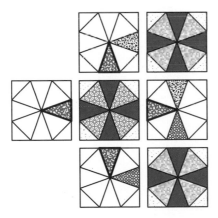

All 4 points should match.

5. Remove the paper from the completed units. Join 2 identical Unit A foundations as shown below to make

each Block A. Staystitch ⅛" from the edge of each block to stabilize the bias edges.

Make 32.

6. Join pairs of Unit B foundations to make the B blocks. Carefully arrange the star-point fabrics so they match the Unit A blocks. Make 14 of Block B with 1 blade of the border print positioned as shown. Staystitch ⅛" from the edge of each block to stabilize the bias edges.

Make 17.   Make 14.

QUILT TOP ASSEMBLY AND FINISHING

1. Arrange the blocks in 9 rows of 7 blocks each, alternating Blocks A and B. Place the 14 B blocks with the border-print piece around the outside edges of the quilt as shown.

2. Add the C and D sections and the corner-block sections around the edges as shown. Sew the blocks into rows. Press the seam allowances in opposite directions from row to row. Sew the rows together.

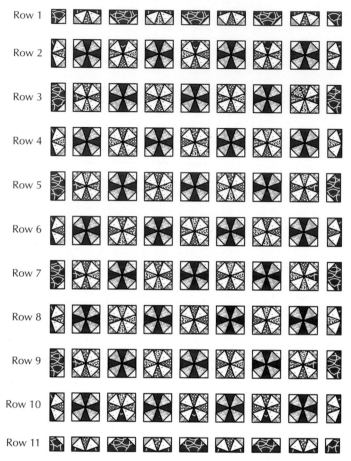

Row 1
Row 2
Row 3
Row 4
Row 5
Row 6
Row 7
Row 8
Row 9
Row 10
Row 11

3. Measure the quilt top for straight-cut borders. Sew the 6½" x 70½" chintz strips to opposite side edges of the quilt top; press the seams, and all following seams, toward the border.

4. Add the 6½" x 68½" chintz border strips to the top and bottom edges.

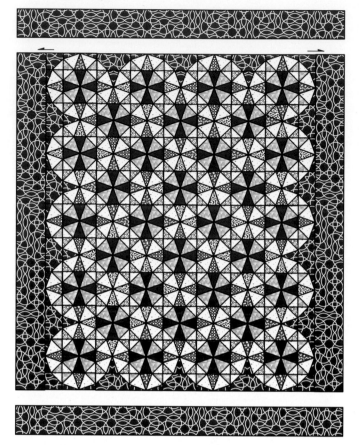

5. Mark the quilting design of your choice on the quilt top; see our suggestion below. Layer the quilt top with batting and backing; baste. Quilt on the marked lines. Bind the edges and add a label.

Mariner's Garden

Quiltmaker:	Virginia Anderson
	Shoreline, Washington
Quilt size:	67" x 67"
Block size:	13" x 13"

Virginia used a variation of the Mariner's Compass design called Compass Flower. When she realized the color placement in one block was different from the others and she contemplated the unpleasant task of ripping out a perfectly good block, Virginia hit upon the wonderful solution of making three more blocks like it. After she completed her quilt, she saw a similar one in Quilters' Newsletter Magazine *made by Judy Mathieson.*

MATERIALS: *44"-wide fabric*

3½ yds. muslin for background
⅞ yd. total assorted red prints for blocks and appliqué
¾ yd. total assorted medium blue prints for blocks and appliqué
¾ yd. total assorted dark blue prints for blocks and appliqué
¼ yd. total assorted gray prints for blocks
¼ yd. total assorted navy blue prints for blocks
2⅛ yds. navy blue stripe for border and sashing*
4 yds. for backing
71" x 71" piece of batting
⅔ yd. for binding

*If the stripe is wider than 3", you may need to purchase more fabric.

UNIT CONSTRUCTION

1. Make 104 photocopies of the Mariner's Garden foundation on the pullout.
2. Referring to "Mariner's Compass" on page 8, construct 104 units. Use 2 different red prints and 2 different blue prints for each block. Make 8 units for each block. Make 4 units with 1 red print in position 4, and 1 light blue print in position 5. Make the other 4 units with a second medium blue print in position 4 and a second red print in position 5. Use 8 rectangles of the same navy blue print for position 1.

Make 4 for each block.   Make 4 for each block.

3. Trim around the outside edges of the foundations.
4. Arrange 8 units as shown above right, alternating the colors. Remove the paper from the right and left edges of each foundation, leaving the rest of the paper intact.

CUTTING

🌸 *Note:* If you cut border strips before constructing the quilt top, cut the strips a little longer than required and trim to fit when you add them to the quilt top.

Use patterns 1–9 on the pullout to make templates. Add ¼"-wide seam allowances to all appliqué pieces.

From the muslin, cut:

2 squares, each 19⅝" x 19⅝"; cut each square twice diagonally for 8 side setting triangles ⊠ ⊠
2 squares, each 10⅛" x 10⅛"; cut each square once diagonally for 4 corner triangles ◹ ◸
52 Template 1
208 Template 2

From the assorted red prints, cut:

26 strips, each 2" x 16"
16 Template 5
8 Template 8

From the assorted medium blue prints, cut:

32 strips, each 2" x 16"
24 Template 4
12 Template 7

From the assorted dark blue prints, cut:

13 strips, each 3" x 17"; crosscut 8 rectangles, each 2" x 3", from each strip for position 1 in the foundations
8 Template 6
4 Template 9

From the assorted gray prints, cut:

26 Template 3

From the assorted navy blue prints, cut:

26 Template 3

From the lengthwise grain of the navy blue stripe, cut:

4 strips, each 3¼" x 88", for the border*
2 strips, each 2" x 74½", for the sashing**
2 strips, each 2" x 45½", for the sashing**
2 strips, each 2" x 16½", for the sashing**
18 strips, each 2" x 13½", for the sashing**

*If your stripe is narrower or wider than 2¾" finished, you will need to adjust the width and length of your border strips.

**If your stripe is narrower or wider than 1½" finished, you will need to adjust the width and the length of your sashing strips.

Sew pairs of units together along the red edge to make 4 sections.

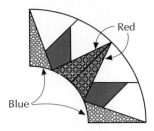

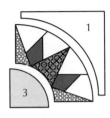

Note: Nine of the Compass blocks have blue points in the north/south positions and 4 blocks have red points in those positions. For the former, join wedges in pairs along the red points; for the latter, join them along the blue points.

5. Stitch a quarter circle (Template 3) to each section. Add a Template 1 piece to the outside edge. Square up each unit if necessary, trimming along the outside edge of the paper foundations.

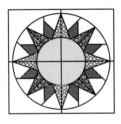

6. Arrange 4 sections as shown and sew them together.

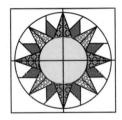

Make 9.　　　　Make 4.

7. Using the templates on the pullout, cut the following paper foundations:

24　Template　4　(Leaf)
16　Template　5　(Teardrop)
8　Template　6　(Circle)
12　Template　7　(Leaf)
8　Template　8　(Teardrop)
4　Template　9　(Circle)

8. Paper patch the above foundations, using the appropriate fabrics. Appliqué pieces 4, 5, and 6 to the side setting triangles and pieces 7, 8, and 9 to the corner triangles as shown.

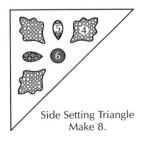

Side Setting Triangle
Make 8.

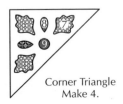

Corner Triangle
Make 4.

QUILT TOP ASSEMBLY AND FINISHING

1. Arrange the blocks, sashing strips, and side setting and corner triangles as shown in the quilt plan below.
2. Sew the blocks together in diagonal rows. Sew the rows together. Add corner triangles last. Trim the ends of the sashing strips even with the edges of the triangles.

3. Measure the quilt top for mitered borders. Add borders to all 4 edges of the quilt top; miter the corners.
4. Mark the top with the design of your choice. See our suggestion below. Layer the quilt top with batting and backing; baste. Quilt on the marked lines. Bind the edges and add a label.

Mariner's Compass

Quiltmaker:	Judy Pollard, 1994
	Seattle, Washington
Quilt size:	68" x 85"
Block size:	13" x 13"
Quilted by:	Hazel Montague

A sprinkling of Liberty of London fabrics adds sparkle to this quilt. The flowered centers of the compasses soften the angles, and the circular quilting suggests a lighthouse beacon. The blue and green sashing adds many different images to this straightforward set of twelve Mariner's Compass blocks.

5 yds. total assorted white prints for background
½ yd. total assorted dark green prints for blocks
½ yd. total assorted medium green prints for blocks and sashing
½ yd. total assorted light green prints for blocks
½ yd. total assorted dark blue prints for blocks
½ yd. total assorted light blue prints for blocks
1¼ yds. total of 2 green prints for sashing strips
2½ yds. large-scale multicolored floral print for borders, sashing and block centers
5 yds. for backing
72" x 89" piece of batting
⅝ yd. for binding

UNIT CONSTRUCTION

1. Make 48 photocopies of Mariner's Compass foundation A and 48 photocopies of foundation B on the pullout. Using Template 3 on the pullout, make 12 paperpatch foundations.
2. Arrange the compass foundations in a circle. Referring to the photo on page 40 and the illustrations below, mark your color choices on each position 4 and 5. In each block, the A foundations will have dark blue in position 5 and light green in position 4; the B foundations will have light blue in position 5 and medium green in position 4.
3. Referring to "Mariner's Compass" on page 8, construct eight compass sections.

Foundation A
Make 4 for
each block.

Foundation B
Make 4 for
each block.

CUTTING

Note: If you cut border strips before constructing the quilt top, cut the strips a little longer than required and trim to fit when you add them to the quilt top.

Use patterns 1–6 on the pullout to make templates.

From the assorted white prints, cut:

48 Template 1 for the blocks
192 Template 2 for the blocks
34 Template 5 for the sashing
14 Template 6 and 14 Template 6 reversed for the sashing
14 rectangles, each 6½" x 13½", for the inner border
4 squares, each 6½" x 6½", for the inner border

From the assorted dark green prints, cut:

a total of 96 rectangles, each 1¾" x 3½"; cut 8 rectangles from the same fabric for each block

From the assorted medium green prints, cut

a total of 48 rectangles, each 2¼" x 5"; cut 4 rectangles from the same fabric for each block

From the assorted light green prints, cut:

48 rectangles, each 2¼" x 5"; cut 4 rectangles from the same fabric for each block

From the assorted dark blue prints, cut:

48 rectangles, each 2¼" x 5¾"; cut 4 rectangles from the same fabric for each block

From the assorted light blue prints, cut:

48 rectangles, each 2¼" x 5¾"; cut 4 rectangles from the same fabric for each block

From the green prints for the sashing, cut:

48 Template 4
4 strips, each 2½" x 42", for the inner border; cut all 4 strips from the same fabric. Crosscut 1 strip into 4 rectangles, each 2½" x 6½", and 2 squares, each 2½" x 2½".

From the floral print, cut:

12 Template 3 (Add ¼"-wide seam allowances.)
4 strips, each 2½" x 42", for the inner border. Crosscut 1 strip into 4 rectangles, each 2½" x 6½", and 2 squares, each 2½" x 2½".
8 strips, each 3" x 42", for the outer border

4. Join pairs of units along the #4 side to form quarter-circles, first removing the paper from the edges to be sewn.

Make 4 for each block.

❀ *Note:* To create a strong north-south orientation for the compass points, sew two #4 sides together to make the quarter-circles. Sewing two #5 sides together will yield an **X** configuration.

Units sewn together   Units sewn together
along the #4 edge   along the #5 edge

5. Fold a white piece 1 in half and mark the center. Pin piece 1 to a quarter-circle, matching the centers. Pin both ends. Pin the rest of the seam, then sew. Press the seam allowance toward the white piece. Repeat for all 4 quarter-units.

6. Remove the remaining paper and square up this section of the block. Sew the 4 quarter-units together.

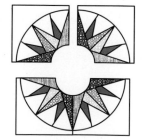

7. Referring to "Paper-Patch Appliqué" on page 11, paper-patch a floral circle (Template 3), then appliqué it to the center to complete the block.

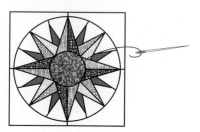

8. To make sashing strips, arrange 2 piece 4 and 2 piece 5 as shown below. Sew them together.

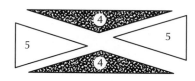 

Make 17.

9. Arrange 1 piece 6, 1 piece 6 reversed, and 1 piece 4 as shown. Sew them together to make half-width sashing strips.

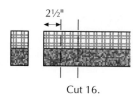

Make 14.

QUILT TOP ASSEMBLY AND FINISHING

1. Sew the green and floral sashing strips together in pairs to make 3 strip sets. Crosscut 1 strip set at 2½" intervals to make 16 segments. Sew 6 pairs of segments together to make four-patch units for the cornerstones. You will have 4 segments left over.

Make 3.

2½"

Cut 16.   Make 6.

2. Cut the 2 remaining strips sets into 10 segments, each 6½" wide, and 6 segments, each 2½" wide. You will have a total of ten 2½"-wide segments.

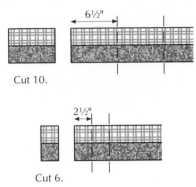

6½"

Cut 10.

2½"

Cut 6.

3. Referring to the photo on page 40, arrange all the units, rectangles, and 2½" green squares in rows. Sew the units into rows; press seam allowances in opposite directions from row to row. Sew the rows together.

4. Sew pairs of 3"-wide floral border strips together to make borders long enough for the quilt.

5. Measure the quilt top for straight-cut borders. Trim 2 border strips to fit the top and bottom edges of the quilt top and sew them to the quilt. Press the seam allowances toward the border.

6. Trim the 2 remaining border strips to fit and sew them to opposite side edges of the quilt top.

7. Mark the quilting design of your choice on the quilt top. See our suggestion below. Layer the quilt top with batting and backing; baste. Quilt on the marked lines. Bind the edges and add a label.

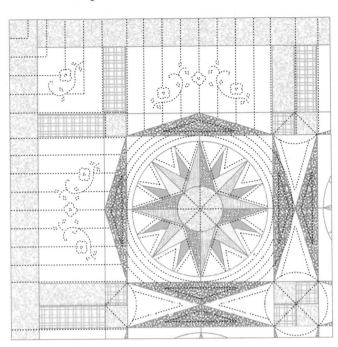

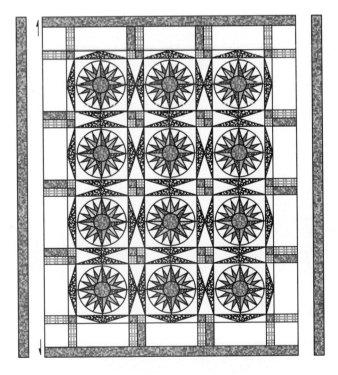

Feathered World Without End

Quiltmaker:	Tricia Lund, 1994
	Seattle, Washington
Quilt size:	63½" x 77½"
Block size:	14" x 14"
Quilted by:	Mrs. John Lehman

If you've always wanted to make a Feathered World Without End quilt but couldn't get enough variety in the feathers with the usual method of strip construction, foundation piecing is the answer to your dilemma. This quilt features an abundance of fabrics, and the pink background and Fan quilting motif unify the different elements.

The predominantly pink-and-blue scraps are balanced by the extensive use of dark and neutral colors. Each block contains between eleven and sixteen fabrics, the majority of which are geometrics. The inner border of teeth is divided into lengths that take their colors from the blocks they adjoin, so that the block colors seem to march around the quilt.

MATERIALS: *44"-wide fabric*

2 yds. total assorted medium and dark prints for large triangles and block centers

2⅞ yds. pink print for background

3 yds. total assorted light prints for small triangles

2¾ yds. total assorted dark prints for small triangles

¼ yd. total assorted pink prints for small diamonds

¼ yd. total assorted blue prints for small diamonds

2¼ yds. plaid for outer border and binding

4⅛ yds. for backing

68" x 82" piece of batting

CUTTING

Note: If you cut border strips before constructing the quilt top, cut the strips a little longer than required and trim to fit when you add them to the quilt top.

Use patterns 1–3 on the pullout to make templates.

From the assorted medium & dark prints, cut:

80 Template 1

20 Template 2

From the pink print for the background, cut:

80 Template 3

From the assorted light & dark prints for small triangles, cut:

50 light strips, each 2" x 42"

52 dark strips, each 2" x 42"

From the assorted pink & blue prints, cut:

a total of 8 strips, each 2" x 42"; cut 4 strips from each color

a total of 4 squares, each 1½" x 1½", for the inner border

From the lengthwise grain of the plaid fabric, cut:

2 strips, each 3½" x 72½", for the outer border

2 strips, each 3½" x 64½", for the outer border

UNIT CONSTRUCTION

1. Make 80 photocopies of foundation 1 and 80 photocopies of foundation 2 on the pullout.

2. Referring to "Teeth" on page 9, construct 80 of foundation 1. Refer to the photo on page 44 for color and value placement. Use a dark or medium fabric in position 1, then alternate dark and light fabrics.

   Make 80 of foundation 2. Choose either pink or blue for position 1 (diamond) and a dark fabric for position 2. Alternate dark and light fabrics. Make 40 foundations with pink diamonds and 40 with blue diamonds. Trim the foundations around the outside edge.

Foundation 1 · · · · · · · · · · · · · Make 80.

Foundation 2 · · · · · · · · · · · Make 40 with pink in position 1.
Make 40 with blue in position 1.

3. Arrange 2 Teeth units with a triangle (Template 1) as shown and sew them together. Be sure the bases of the dark teeth are on the outside edge of the unit.

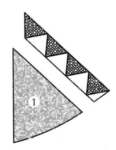 

Make 80.

4. Arrange 4 units with identical diamond fabrics around a center piece (Template 2) as shown. Pin the seams, then sew them together, beginning and ending your stitching ¼" from the end of the seam.

Begin and end stitching
¼" from the edge.

5. Add pink background pieces (Template 3) as shown. Begin the stitching ¼" from the center point, backstitch, and sew to the outside edge. Repeat on the other edge of the triangle.

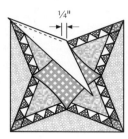

Stitch from the center to edge.

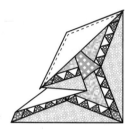

Make 20.

QUILT TOP ASSEMBLY AND FINISHING

1. Make 18 photocopies of the border Teeth foundation on the pullout. Construct each border Teeth unit, using the assorted light and dark 2"-wide strips. Begin and end with light fabric. Match the colors in the strip to the colors in the block it will border. Make 18 foundation units.

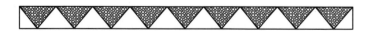

2. Referring to the photo on page 44, arrange the blocks in 5 rows of 4 blocks each. Alternate the pink and blue diamonds. Arrange the border Teeth units and the 1½" corner squares around the edges. Sew the rows together, including the top and bottom row of border teeth and corner squares. Press the seam allowances in opposite directions from row to row. Sew the rows together.

3. Measure the quilt top for straight-cut borders. Trim 2 border strips to fit the sides of the quilt top. Sew them to opposite side edges, pressing the seams toward the border. Repeat for the top and bottom borders.

4. Mark the quilting design of your choice on the quilt top. See our suggestion below. Layer the quilt top with batting and backing; baste. Quilt on the marked lines. Bind the edges and add a label.

Country Roses

Quiltmaker:	Tricia Lund, 1995
	Seattle, Washington
Quilt size:	16" x 16"
Block size:	41½" x 41½"
Quilted by:	Nedra Hall

"Country Roses" is based on the Rose of Sharon appliqué pattern, which has long been popular with quilters. Instead of appliquéd flowers, this version features a central pieced flower surrounded by pieced buds. The only appliquéd components are the leaves and stems.

The somewhat prim pattern is balanced by informal fabrics. If you love a wide variety of fabrics in a quilt, a monochromatic color scheme can be a challenge. Plaids, stripes, and checks enliven the color palette and sedate design.

¾ yd. total assorted medium and dark blue prints for flower centers, teeth, leaves, and corner squares
⅝ yd. total assorted light blue prints and checks for flower centers, teeth, sashing, and corner squares
¾ yd. dark blue check for sashing and stems
⅛ dark blue print for sashing and corner squares
1⅛ yds. white print for background
2⅝ yds. for backing
46" x 46" piece of batting
⅓ yd. for binding
¼"-wide bias bar

CUTTING

Use patterns 1–4 on page 78 to make templates.

From the assorted medium & dark blue prints, cut:

2"-wide strips totaling 256" in length for the teeth
16 Template 1
4 strips from medium prints, each 1½" x 24", for the leaves
4 strips from dark prints, each 1½" x 24", for the leaves
3 strips, 1½" x 29", for the corner squares
3 strips, each 1½" x 15", for the corner squares

From the assorted light blue prints & checks, cut:

16 Template 1
2"-wide strips totaling 192" in length, for the teeth
12 sashing strips, each 1½" x 16½"

From the dark blue check, cut:

24 sashing strips, each 1½" x 16½"
16 bias strips, each 1⅛" x 3½"

From the dark blue print, cut:

2 strips, each 1½" x 29", for the corner squares
1 strip, 1½" x 15", for the corner squares

From the white print, cut:

16 Template 2
16 Template 3
16 rectangles, each 4¾" x 8"

UNIT CONSTRUCTION

1. Make 32 photocopies of the Teeth foundation on page 78.
2. Referring to "Teeth" on page 9, construct 32 units. Use the assorted 2"-wide strips, beginning with a dark fabric. Alternate light and dark in each foundation. Refer to the photo on page 47 for color-placement ideas.

Make 32.

3. Arrange each Teeth unit with a flower center 1. Pin the flower center to the Teeth unit in the center and at both edges. Sew the pieces together with the flower center on top.

 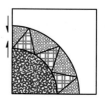

Make 32.

4. Add piece 2 to 16 of the flower units as shown below. To reduce bulk in this seam, carefully trim the seam allowance on the teeth side to about ⅛". Do not trim the piece 1 seam allowance. Press the seam allowance toward the Teeth unit.

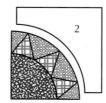

Center Unit
Make 16.

Tip: As you sew around the curve, lengthen the stitch in the middle where the stem will be inserted. Shorten the stitch length again to sew the remainder of the seam. This will make it easier to insert the stem in step 9 on page 49.

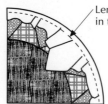

Lengthen the stitches in the middle of the curve.

5. Arrange 4 center units and sew them together.

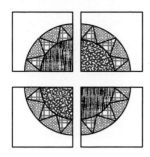

6. Add piece 3 to the 16 remaining flower units as shown. Trim the teeth section to ⅛" as you did for the flower centers. Press seam allowances toward the teeth section.

Flower Unit
Make 16.

7. Arrange 1 center unit with 4 flower units and 4 white 4¾" x 8" rectangles. Alternate the placement of the piece 1 fabrics in the center and at the corners. Refer to the photo on page 47. Sew the pieces into rows, pressing the seams toward the corner flowers. Sew the rows together. To make inserting the stem piece easier, lengthen the stitches at the inside corners (indicated by an X in the illustration).

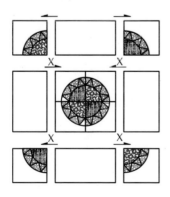

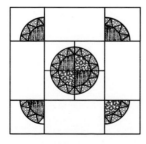

Make 4.

8. Fold each blue-check bias strip in half lengthwise, wrong sides together. Sew with a ¼"-wide seam allowance. (Insert a ¼"-wide bias bar to check fit. If needed, adjust the width of the seam.) Trim the seam allowance to ⅛". Insert the bias bar and rotate the seam to the back. Press.

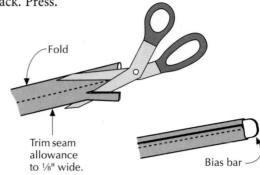

Fold

Trim seam allowance to ⅛" wide.

Bias bar

9. Undo a few stitches at each end of the stem line. Insert a stem and appliqué it in place, catching the unstitched edges of the blocks in the appliqué to hold them in place. Repeat for all 4 corners of each block.

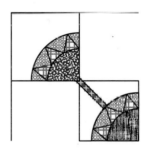

10. Sew the 1½" x 24" leaf strips together in light/medium pairs as shown. Press the seam allowance open. Pin Template 4 to the wrong side of the strip set, placing the line on the template on the stitching line. Cut around the outside of the leaf pattern, adding a ¼"-wide seam allowance. Paper-patch the leaves, then appliqué 8 leaves to each block, referring to the photo on page 47 for placement. Place the darker half of the leaf toward the center flower.

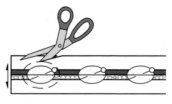

Cut 32 leaves.

QUILT TOP ASSEMBLY AND FINISHING

1. Arrange the blue check and light sashing strips as shown below and sew them together. Press the seam allowances toward the darker fabric.

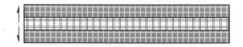

Make 12.

2. Sew the 1½"-wide medium and dark blue strips into strip sets as shown below. Press the seam allowances toward the lighter fabric in each set. Crosscut the strip sets at 1½" intervals.

 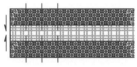

Cut 18.

 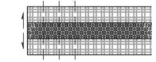

Cut 9.

3. Arrange and sew the segments together. Press the seam allowances as shown.

Make 9.

4. Referring to the photo on page 47, arrange the blocks, sashing strips, and corner squares in rows. Sew the blocks together into rows, pressing the seams toward the sashing strips. Sew the rows together.

5. Mark the quilting design of your choice on the quilt top. See our suggestion below. Layer the quilt top with batting and backing; baste. Quilt on the marked lines. Bind the edges and add a label.

Foundation Stars

Quiltmaker: Judy Pollard, 1995
              Seattle, Washington
Quilt size: 22¾" x 22¾"
Block size: 2" x 2"

This simple two-block quilt allows the fabric to tell the story. The blocks are sewn into rows, creating two star images. The print fabric used for the star centers adds interest and dimension to the design.

MATERIALS: *44"-wide fabric*

⅓ yd. total assorted light blue prints for background

⅔ yd. total assorted dark blue prints for star points, middle border, and binding

⅛ yd. medium blue print for star centers

⅜ yd. floral print for star centers and border

¾ yd. for backing

28" x 28" piece of batting

CUTTING

❀ **Note:** If you cut border strips before constructing the quilt top, cut the strips a little longer than required and trim to fit when you add them to the quilt top.

From the assorted light blue prints, cut:

1 strip, 2½" x 42"; crosscut 16 squares, each 2½" x 2½"

2 strips, each 3½" x 42"; crosscut 24 squares, each 3½" x 3½", for the star point background

2 strips, each 1" x 14½", for the inner border

2 strips, each 1" x 15½", for the inner border

From the assorted dark blue prints, cut:

2 strips, each 4" x 42"; crosscut 48 rectangles, each 1¾" x 4"

2 strips, each 1¼" x 17", for the middle border

2 strips, each 1¼" x 15½", for the middle border

From the medium blue print, cut:

1 strip, 2½" x 42"; crosscut 5 squares, each 2½" x 2½"

From the floral print, cut:

4 squares, each 2½" x 2½"

2 strips, each 4" x 24", for the outer border

2 rectangles, each 4" x 17", for the outer border

UNIT CONSTRUCTION

1. Make 24 photocopies of the Star Point foundation on page 75.

2. Referring to "Flying Geese" on page 6, construct 24 star points. Use the 3½" light blue squares and the 1¾" x 4" dark blue rectangles.

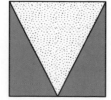

Make 24.

QUILT TOP ASSEMBLY AND FINISHING

1. Arrange the star points and plain squares, referring to the illustration below and the photo on page 51. Sew the units into rows. Press the seam allowances toward the plain squares in each row. Sew the rows together.

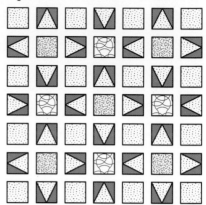

2. Measure the quilt for straight-cut borders. Sew the 1" x 14½" light blue strips to the side edges of the quilt top. Add the 1" x 15½" light blue strips to the top and bottom edges. Press the seam allowances, and all following seams, toward the border.

3. Add the middle and outer borders in the same manner.

4. Mark the quilt top with the quilting design of your choice. See our suggestion below. Layer the quilt top with backing and batting; baste. Quilt on all the marked lines. Bind the edges and add a label.

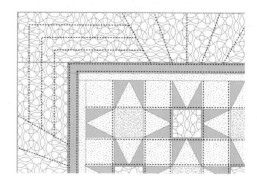

English Geese

Quiltmaker:	Tricia Lund, 1995
	Seattle, Washington
Quilt size:	58" x 58"
Strip size:	3" x 7½"
Quilted by:	Bev Payne

The fabrics chosen for this quilt offered an unusual challenge. The floral print's leaves have a yellow-green cast, and the companion plaid has a strong blue-green component. The two greens looked fine together in the floral fabric, so Tricia selected both yellow-green and blue-green fabrics as candidates for the geese patches. The stacks of fabric sat side by side, eyeing each other suspiciously. When Tricia combined them, some serious clashes resulted, but the blue-green seemed to dominate. After the yellow-greens returned to their shelf, things settled down and peace returned to the quilt.

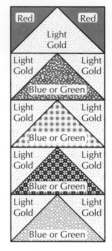

MATERIALS: *44"-wide fabric*

1 yd. total assorted blue and green prints for geese

1½ yds. red print for stars and inner border (⅞ yd. if you cut the borders on the crosswise grain and piece them)

⅛ yd. plaid #1 for Square Within a Square units

⅞ yd. plaid #2 for side triangles and binding

⅜ yd. red check for Square Within a Square units

1⅝ yds. light gold print for Flying Geese background

2¼ yds. large floral print for background squares, side triangles, and outer border (You may need more if you cut specific areas of the fabric for the background squares.)

3¾ yds. for backing

62" x 62" piece of batting

UNIT CONSTRUCTION

1. Make 36 photocopies of the Flying Geese foundation and 13 photocopies of the Square Within a Square foundation on page 77.

2. Referring to "Flying Geese" on page 6, construct 36 units. Use assorted blue and green strips for positions 1, 4, 7, and 10, and the light gold strips for positions 2, 3, 5, 6, 8, 9, 11, 12, and 13. Use red print strips for positions 14 and 15. Refer to the photo on page 53 for color-placement ideas.

Make 36.

CUTTING

Note: If you cut border strips before constructing the quilt top, cut the strips a little longer than required and trim to fit when you add them to the quilt top.

From the assorted blue & green prints, cut:

8 strips, each 2¼" x 42"

From the lengthwise grain of the red print, cut:

2 strips, each 1½" x 44½", for the inner border

2 strips, each 1½" x 46½", for the inner border

9 squares, each 4" x 4", for the Square within a Square centers

6 strips, each 2" x 42"

From plaid #1, cut:

4 squares, each 4" x 4", for the Square within a Square centers

From plaid #2, cut:

2 squares, each 12" x 12". Cut each square twice diagonally for a total of 8 triangles for side setting triangles. (You will have 1 extra triangle.)

From the red check, cut:

3 strips, each 2" x 42"

From the light gold, cut:

19 strips, each 2" x 42", for the Flying Geese units

4 strips, each 2¼" x 42", for position 13 in the Flying Geese units

4 Template 1

8 Template 2

From the lengthwise grain of the large floral print, cut:

2 strips, each 6½" x 46½", for the outer borders

2 strips, each 6½" x 58½", for the outer borders

12 setting squares, each 8" x 8"

2 squares, each 12" x 12"; cut each square twice diagonally for a total of 8 triangles (You will have 3 extra triangles.)

3. Referring to "Square Within a Square" on page 10, construct 9 units, using the 4" red squares for position 1 and the red-check strips for positions 2, 3, 4, and 5. Make 4 units, using 4" plaid #1 squares for position 1 and red-check strips for positions 2, 3, 4, and 5.

Make 9.

Make 4.

4. Remove the paper foundations from all the units.

QUILT TOP ASSEMBLY AND FINISHING

1. Arrange the Flying Geese units, Square Within a Square units, and the remaining squares and triangles into diagonal rows as shown below.
2. Sew the blocks into rows, pressing the seams in the direction of the arrows. Sew the rows together.

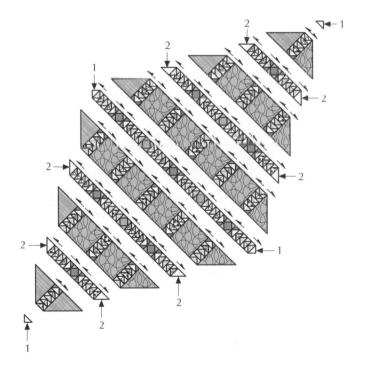

3. Measure the quilt top for straight-cut borders. Sew the 1½" x 44½" inner-border strips to opposite side edges. Add the 1½" x 46½" inner-border strips to the top and bottom edges. Press these seams, and all following seams, toward the border.
4. Add outer-border strips in the same manner.

5. Mark the quilting design of your choice on the quilt top. See our suggestion below. Layer the quilt top with batting and backing; baste. Quilt on the marked lines. Bind the edges and add a label.

Old-Fashioned Log Cabin

Quiltmaker:	Tricia Lund, 1992
	Seattle, Washington
Quilt size:	77" x 77"
Block size:	12¾" x 12¾"
Quilted by:	The Amish

Reminiscent of the dark utilitarian quilts of the late nineteenth century, this Log Cabin design features mostly geometric and solid-looking prints. Bias-cut checks and plaids and crosswise, lengthwise, and even bias-cut striped fabrics are all utilized.

Notice that the shading in each block is divided diagonally as well as into concentric rings. A ring of light and medium-light fabrics alternates with a ring of medium-dark and dark fabrics. Sometimes the first ring around the red chimney block is the lighter combination and sometimes the darker. Unlike most Log Cabin quilts, there is no consistent pattern of diagonal shading.

MATERIALS: *44"-wide fabric*

½ yd. red print for center squares (chimneys)
7½ yds. total assorted light, medium, and dark prints in red, blue, brown, and black for logs
5 yds. for backing
81" x 81" piece of batting
⅔ yd. for binding

CUTTING

From the red print for the center squares, cut:

4 strips, each 3½" x 42"; crosscut 36 squares, each 3½" x 3½"

From the assorted prints for logs, cut:

36 strips, each 2" x 28", for logs 1, 2, 9, and 10
36 strips, each 2" x 33", for logs 3, 4, 11, and 12
36 strips, each 2" x 38", for logs 5, 6, 13, and 14
36 strips, each 2" x 43", for logs 7, 8, 15, and 16

UNIT CONSTRUCTION

1. Make 36 photocopies of the Log Cabin foundation on the pullout, or trace it onto muslin or large sheets of paper.
2. Referring to "Log Cabin" on page 8, construct 36 blocks. Refer to the photo on page 56 for shading and color-placement ideas.

Note: In her quilt, Tricia alternated light and dark fabrics for each round. She used 1 light and 1 dark on 1 side of the block, and the other light and dark on the other side of the block.

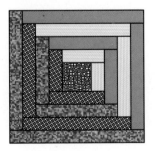

QUILT TOP ASSEMBLY AND FINISHING

1. Arrange the blocks into rows as shown. Sew the rows together, pressing the seam allowances in opposite directions from row to row.

2. Layer the quilt top with batting and backing; baste. Quilt as desired, or follow our quilting suggestion below. Bind the edges and add a label.

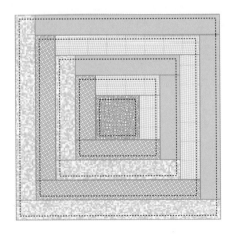

Teresa's Wedding Quilt

Quiltmaker: Judy Pollard, 1995
Seattle, Washington
Quilt size: 54" x 67"
Block size: 8" x 8"
Quilted by: Gretchen Engle

Judy had great fun designing this Basket block so she could foundation piece it. The quilt's energy, exuberance, and color remind her of her friend Teresa. The four-patch units in the corners create a strong diagonal line, which is accentuated by the quilting.

MATERIALS: *44"-wide fabric*

3½ yds. dark blue print for borders and background
1¾ yds. total assorted bold-colored prints for baskets and
   cornerstones
1 yd. medium blue stripe for sashing
3⅓ yds. for backing
58" x 71" piece of batting
½ yd. for binding

CUTTING

Note: If you cut border strips before constructing the quilt top, cut the strips a little longer than required and trim to fit when you add them to the quilt top.

Use the pattern on page 73 to make Template 1.

From the lengthwise grain of the dark blue print, cut:

2 strips, each 8½" x 42½"
2 strips, each 6½" x 67½"
10 squares, each 4⅞" x 4⅞"; cut each square once diagonally
   for 20 triangles (1 for each block)
40 squares, each 2½" x 2½", 2 for each block
20 squares, each 2⅞" x 2⅞"; cut each square once diagonally
   for 40 triangles (2 for each block)
80 rectangles, 1½" x 3", for the end teeth shapes (4 for each
   block)
40 Template 1 for the middle teeth shapes (2 for each block)
20 strips, each 1½" x 13", for the four-patch units (1 for each
   block)
15 strips, each 1½" x 6½", for the cornerstones

From the assorted bold-colored prints, cut*:

10 squares, each 4⅞" x 4⅞"; cut each square once diagonally
   for 20 triangles (1 for each block)
20 squares, each 2⅞" x 2⅞"; cut each square once diagonally
   for 40 triangles (2 for each block)
80 Template 1 for middle teeth shapes (4 for each block)
20 strips, each 1½" x 13", for the four-patch units (1 for each
   block)
15 strips, each 1½" x 6½", for the cornerstones

Cut all the pieces for each basket from the same fabric.

From the medium blue stripe, cut:

49 strips, each 2½" x 8½", for the sashing

UNIT CONSTRUCTION

1. Make 40 photocopies of the Teeth foundation on page 73. Referring to "Teeth" on page 9, construct 40 units. Use the dark blue and bold-colored prints. Using the same fabric for each block, make 2 units.

2. Sew the 1½" x 13" bold print and dark blue strips together. Make 20 strip sets, pressing the seam allowances toward the darker fabric. Crosscut 8 segments, each 1½" wide, from each strip set. Sew pairs of segments together to make 4 four-patch units for each block.

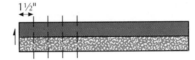

Make 80.

3. Sew each large dark blue triangle to a large bold-print triangle. Repeat with the small dark blue and bold-print triangles.

4. Arrange all the units for 1 block as shown, taking care that the four-patch units face in the proper direction. Sew the units into rows, pressing the seams as shown. Sew the rows together.

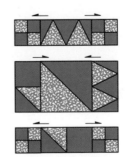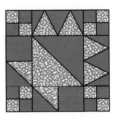

Quilt Top Assembly and Finishing

1. Sew the 1½" x 6½" dark blue and bold print strips together. Press the seam allowances toward the darker fabric. Cut the strip sets into 1½"-wide segments. Sew pairs of segments together to make 30 four-patch units for the cornerstones.

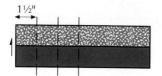

Make 30.

2. Referring to the photo on page 58, arrange the blocks, sashing strips, and cornerstones in rows. Make sure to arrange the four-patch cornerstones so they continue the diagonal line of the four-patch corners in the blocks.

3. Sew the blocks and sashing strips into rows. Press the seam allowances toward the sashing strips. Sew the rows together.

4. Measure the quilt top for top and bottom borders. Sew the 8½" x 42½" strips to the top and bottom edges of the quilt top.

5. Add the 6½" x 67½" strips to opposite side edges of the quilt top.

6. Mark the quilting design of your choice on the quilt top. See our suggestion below Layer the quilt top with batting and backing; baste. Quilt on the marked lines. Bind the edges and add a label.

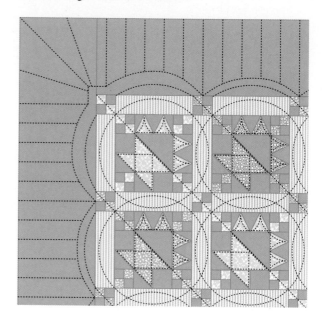

Blue Danube

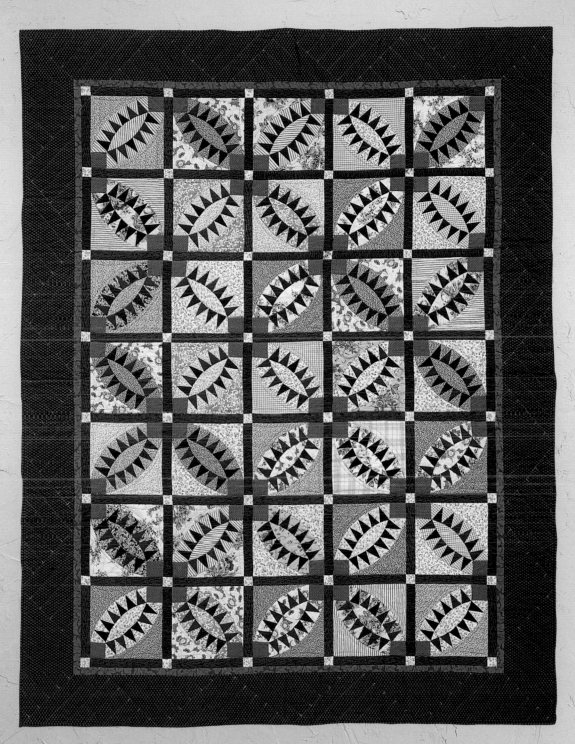

Quiltmaker:	Judy Pollard, 1995
	Seattle, Washington
Quilt size:	59½" x 76½"
Block size:	8" x 8"
Quilted by:	Gretchen Engle

A delightful shopping spree at a local quilt show supplied many of the seventeen background fabrics in this quilt. Teeth units in several shades of dark blue unify the design and add to the scrappy, informal look. Judy cut each template shape from several sets of fabric, then mixed and matched them for both light and dark blocks. She alternated the light and dark blocks, adding dimension to the quilt.

MATERIALS: *44"-wide fabric*

4 yds. total assorted light and medium blue prints for
   background and cornerstones
2 yds. navy blue solid for blocks
⅓ yd. bright blue print for corner squares
1 yd. dark blue print #1 for sashing
2 yds. dark blue print #2 for outer border (If you cut these
   borders on the crosswise grain and piece them, 1⅓ yds.
   is sufficient.)
¼ yd. medium blue print for inner border
3½ yds. for backing
64" x 81" piece of batting
⅝ yd. for binding

CUTTING

Note: If you cut border strips before constructing
the quilt top, cut the strips a little longer than required and trim to fit when you add them to the
quilt top.

Use patterns 1 and 2 on the pullout to make templates.

From the *assorted light & medium blue prints*, cut:

a total of 70 Template 1 (corner)
a total of 35 Template 2 (melon)
a total of 70 strips, each 2" x 42" (You need 2 strips of the
   same fabric for each block.)
2 strips, each 1½" x 42"; crosscut 48 squares, each 1½" x 1½",
   for the cornerstones

From the *navy blue solid*, cut:

33 strips, each 2" x 42"

From the *bright blue print*, cut:

70 squares, each 2¼" x 2¼"

From the *lengthwise grain* of *dark blue print #1*, cut:

4 strips, each 8½" x 31½"; crosscut 82 strips, each 1½" x 8½"

From the *lengthwise grain* of *dark blue print #2*, cut:

2 strips, each 6" x 66"
2 strips, each 6" x 59"

From the *medium blue print for the inner border*, cut:

6 strips, each 1¼" x 42"

UNIT CONSTRUCTION

1. Make 70 photocopies of the Teeth foundation on the
   pullout.
2. Referring to "Teeth" on page 9, construct 70 arcs. Use
   the navy blue solid in positions 2, 4, 6, 8, 10, and 12.
   Use 1 light or medium print in the remaining spots.
   Use the same print for each pair. Refer to the photo on
   page 61 for color-placement ideas.

3. Sew each arc to a corner piece (Template 1), matching
   the center and both ends of the curved seam. Press the
   seam allowance toward the corner piece.

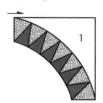

4. Sew a 2¼" bright blue square to each end of 35 arcs.
   Press the seam allowances toward the blue square.

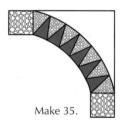

Make 35.

5. Add a melon (Template 2) to this unit, stopping and
   starting the stitching at the intersection of the arc and
   the square. Press the seam allowance toward the arc.

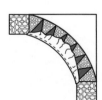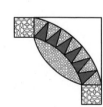

6. Sew another corner unit to the melon, stopping and starting the stitching at the intersection of the arc and the square. Choose 2 arcs made with the same light background print for each block. Press the seam allowance toward the arc.

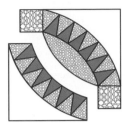

7. Sew the remaining seams between the end squares and the arcs. Press the seam allowance toward the end square.

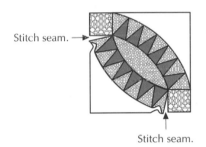 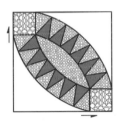

Stitch seam. →

Stitch seam.

QUILT TOP ASSEMBLY AND FINISHING

1. Referring to the photo on page 61, arrange the blocks, sashing strips, and cornerstones.
2. Sew the units together in rows, pressing seams toward the sashing strips. Sew the rows together.
3. Cut two 1¼"-wide medium blue strips in half crosswise. Sew 1 piece to each of the 4 remaining strips. Measure the quilt top for straight-cut borders. Trim the 2 longer strips to fit the side edges and sew them to the quilt top. Press the seam allowances, and all remaining seams, toward the borders. Trim the 2 remaining strips to fit and add them to the top and bottom edges of the quilt top in the same manner.
4. Sew the 6" x 66" dark blue strips to opposite side edges of the quilt top. Add the 6" x 59" dark blue strips to the top and bottom edges.

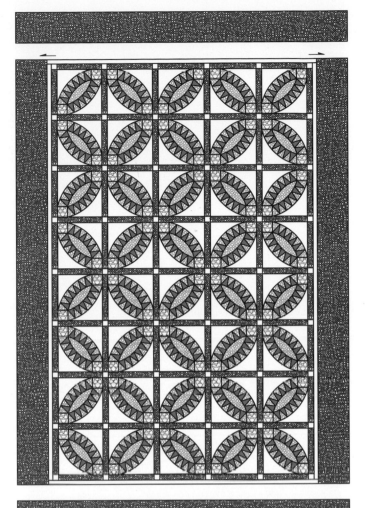

7. Mark the quilting design of your choice on the quilt top. See our suggestion below. Layer the quilt top with batting and backing; baste. Quilt on the marked lines. Bind the edges and add a label.

Pickled Cherries

Quiltmakers:	Judy Pollard & Tricia Lund, 1993 Seattle, Washington
Quilt size:	46" x 46"
Quilted by:	Teresa Haskins

Some ideas come after much mulling over, but others spring forth so enthusiastically that a quiltmaker can only stand back and bow to the quilt's wishes. From the moment it was finished, this center design shouted for a cherry border. The cherries just had to be various shades of red, and even though stems and leaves are usually green, this quilt demanded the black and beige check, which persisted through auditions of numerous other fabrics. This piece illustrates our first rule of quilt design—be sure to listen, for your quilt may be talking to you.

Tricia chose the fabrics and appliquéd the border, and Judy pieced the Pickle Dish center of this delightful quilt.

MATERIALS: *44"-wide fabric*

2⅝ yds. total assorted beige prints for background and outer border (1½ yds. required for the border)
1 yd. total assorted dark prints for blocks
⅞ yd. total assorted light prints for blocks
⅛ yd. light gray print for blocks
¼ yd. bright blue print for inner border
¼ yd. total assorted red prints for cherries
1 yd. black check for stems and leaves
3 yds. for backing (or add 6"-wide borders to opposite side edges of 1½ yds. backing)
50" x 50" piece of batting
½ yd. for binding
⅛"- and ¼"-wide bias bars

UNIT CONSTRUCTION

1. Make 32 photocopies of the Teeth foundation on the pullout. Referring to "Teeth" on page 9, construct 32 arcs. Use the dark and light print rectangles.

2. Mark the center of each long edge of each pieced arc and the center of the curved edge of each template piece.

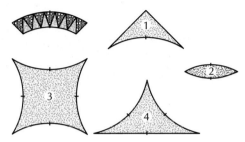

CUTTING

Note: If you cut border strips before constructing the quilt top, cut the strips a little longer than required and trim to fit when you add them to the quilt top.

Use patterns 1–8 on the pullout to make templates. Add ¼"-wide seam allowances to all appliqué pieces.

*From the **lengthwise grain** of the assorted beige prints, cut:*

4 strips, each 7½" x 46½", for the border

From the remaining beige prints, cut:

16 squares, each 2¼" x 2¼"   5 Template 3 for centers
4 Template 1 for corners   4 Template 4 for side units
16 Template 2 (melon)

Cutting Diagram
Cut Templates 1– 4
from fabric as shown.

From the assorted dark prints, cut:

224 rectangles, each 2" x 2¾" (or 2"-wide strips to total 616" in length)

From the assorted light prints, cut:

192 rectangles, each 2" x 2¾" (or 2"-wide strips to total 528" in length)

From the gray print , cut:

16 squares, each 2¼" x 2¼"

From the bright blue print, cut:

4 strips, each 1" x 42"

From the assorted red prints, cut:

72 cherries (Use Template 5 as a guide, but make each cherry a little different in size and shape.)

From the black check, cut:

72 leaves (12 each from Templates 6, 6r, 7, 7r, 8, and 8r)
16 bias strips, each 1⅛" x 7", for the side vines
8 bias strips, each 1⅛" x 9", for the corner vines
24 bias strips, each ⅞" x 8½", for the cherry stems

3. Pin an arc to 1 side of each melon piece, matching centers and corners. Stitch, pressing the seam toward the melon piece (Template 2).

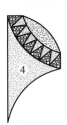 *Note:* To sew curved seams, match centers and ends of the melons and foundation. Sew slowly, adjusting the seam edges as necessary. Stitch with the melon piece on top.

Make 16.

4. Sew a melon-arc unit to 2 adjacent sides of a center piece (Template 3). Press the seam allowance toward the arc.

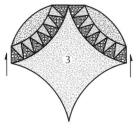

Make 5.

5. Add melon-arc units to 3 side units (Template 4) and 2 corner units (Template 1) as shown below.

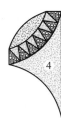 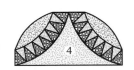

Make 1.   Make 1.   Make 1.

Make 1.   Make 1.

6. Sew a 2¼" gray square to each end of 8 arcs. Add a beige square to each end of the 8 remaining arcs.

Make 8.   Make 8.

7. Sew an arc with gray squares to an arc with beige squares. Make 6 units.

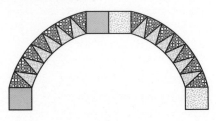

Make 6.

8. Add a completed arc unit to the bottom side piece and to each center piece. Sew with the arc on top, pinning in the center and at both ends, matching seams as shown. Do not stretch or pull while sewing.

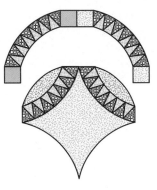 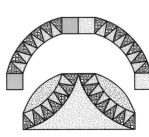

Make 5.   Make 1.

9. Sew arcs with beige squares to the left side and left corner pieces as shown. Add the arcs with gray squares to the right corner and right side pieces.

Make 1 of each.

QUILT TOP ASSEMBLY AND FINISHING

1. Arrange all the units as shown and sew them together in numerical order.

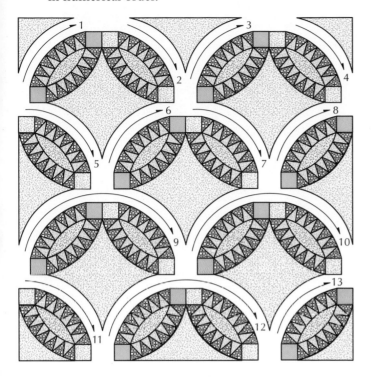

2. Pin each blue border strip to a beige border strip, matching the centers. Stitch. Press the seam allowances toward the blue strip.

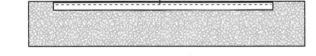

3. Measure the quilt top for mitered borders. Pin the border strips to the quilt top, matching the center of each side of the quilt top to the center of each border strip. Sew the borders in place; start and stop stitching ¼" from the edge of the quilt top. Miter the corners.

4. Using the 1⅛" x 7" and 1⅛" x 9" bias strips of black check and a ¼"-wide bias bar, construct ¼"-wide bias vines. (See "Country Roses," on pages 47–50.) Repeat with the ⅞" x 8½" bias strips and a ⅛"-wide bias bar to make cherry stems. Trim seam allowances so they do not show on the front side when they are pressed. Cut each cherry-stem piece into 3 pieces of equal length.

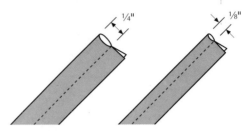

5. Transfer the border appliqué design (on the pullout) to all 4 borders. Arrange the 9"-long bias strips in the corners and the 7"-long bias strips around the edges to form the vine; arrange 3 cherry stems between each vine segment. Appliqué them in place.

6. Cut paper foundations for 72 cherries (Template 5) and 72 leaves (12 each of Templates 6, 6r, 7, 7r, 8, and 8r). Paper-patch the leaves and cherries. Arrange them around the border, referring to the photo on page 64. Note that the cherry/leaf clusters alternate direction as they move around the quilt. Appliqué them in place.

7. Mark the quilting design of your choice on the quilt top. See our suggestion below. Layer the quilt top with batting and backing; baste. Quilt on the marked lines. Bind the edges and add a label.

Heidi's Wedding Quilt

Quiltmaker:	Judy Pollard, 1995
	Seattle, Washington
Quilt size:	46" x 46"
Quilted by:	Gretchen Engle

The Double Wedding Ring is a traditional design. A book on antique quilts gave Judy the inspiration for Heidi's quilt, and fabric with a country feel seemed right for a farm family. The borders became a "design decision" after Judy realized she had cut the original border strips too small. The end result is pleasing indeed.

MATERIALS: *44"-wide fabric*

1¾ yds. total assorted red prints for background and borders
1 yd. total assorted dark and light prints for ring segments
¼ yd. brown stripe for melons
⅛ yd. gold print for blocks
⅛ yd. red print for blocks
¼ yd. blue print for inner border
3 yds. for backing (or add 6"-wide borders to both side edges of 1½ yds. backing fabric)
50" x 50" piece of batting
½ yd. for binding

UNIT CONSTRUCTION

1. Make 32 photocopies of the Wedding Ring foundation on the pullout. Referring to "Fan" on page 7, construct 32 arcs. Use the assorted dark and light prints 2" x 2¾" rectangles.

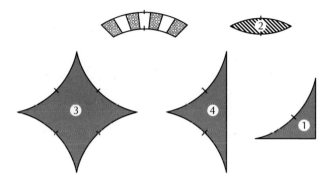

2. Mark the center of each arc and the center of the curved edge of each template piece.

CUTTING

❀ **Note:** If you cut border strips before constructing the quilt top, cut the strips a little longer than required and trim to fit when you add them to the quilt top.

Use patterns 1–4 on the pullout to make templates.

From the lengthwise grain of the assorted red prints, cut:

4 strips, each 6" x 32½", for the borders

From the remaining assorted red prints, cut:

4 squares, each 6" x 6"
5 Template 3 for centers
4 Template 4 for side pieces
4 Template 1 for corners

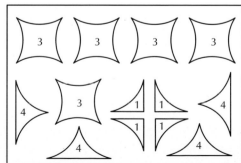

Cutting Diagram
Cut Templates 1–3
from fabric as shown.

From the assorted dark & light prints, cut:

224 rectangles, each 2" x 2¾"

From the brown stripe, cut:

16 Template 2

From the gold print, cut:

16 squares, each 2¼" x 2¼"

From the red print for blocks, cut:

16 squares, each 2¼" x 2¼"

From the blue print, cut:

5 strips, each 1½" x 42". Cut 1 strip in half and sew 1 piece to each of 2 long strips. Then crosscut 2 strips, each 1½" x 45½"; 2 strips, each 1½" x 32½"; and 4 strips, each 1½" x 6".

3. Pin an arc to one side of each melon piece (Template 2), matching centers and corners. Stitch, pressing the seam toward the melon.

Make 16.

 **Note:** To sew curved seams, match centers and ends of the melons and foundation. Sew slowly, adjusting the seam edges as necessary.

4. Sew a melon-arc unit to 2 adjacent sides of a center piece (Template 3). Press the seam allowance toward the arc.

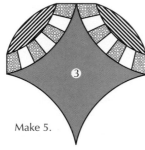

Make 5.

5. Add melon-arc units to 3 side units (Template 4) and 2 corner units (Template 1) as shown.

Make 1.   Make 1.   Make 1.

Make 1.   Make 1.

6. Sew a 2¼" gold square to each end of 8 arcs. Add a red square to each end of the 8 remaining arcs.

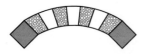 

7. Sew an arc with gold squares to the right edge of an arc with red squares. Make 6 units.

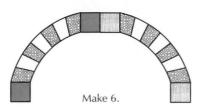

Make 6.

8. Add a completed arc unit to the bottom side piece and each center piece. Sew with the arc on top, pinning in the center and at both ends. Do not stretch or pull while sewing.

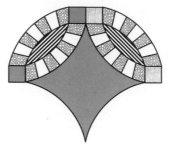 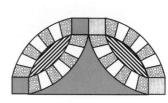

Make 5.   Make 1.

9. Sew arcs with gold squares to the left corner and left side pieces as shown. Sew arcs with red squares to the right corner and right side pieces.

Make 1 of each.

QUILT TOP ASSEMBLY AND FINISHING

1. Arrange the units as shown below and sew them together in numerical order.

2. Measure the quilt top for top and bottom borders. Sew the 1½" x 32½" blue and the 6" x 32½" red borders to the top and bottom edges of the quilt top as shown. Press the seam allowances toward the borders.

3. Arrange the reserved red border strips with the 1½" x 6" blue strips and the 6" red squares. Sew them together as shown to make 2 side borders. Press the seam allowances toward the center.

Make 2.

4. Measure the quilt top for side borders. Add the 1½" x 45½" blue strips to opposite side edges of the quilt top, then add the pieced border strips as shown. Press the seam allowances toward the borders.

5. Mark the quilting design of your choice on the quilt top. See our suggestion below. Layer the quilt top with batting and backing; baste. Quilt on the marked lines. Bind the edges and add a label.

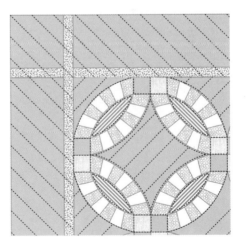

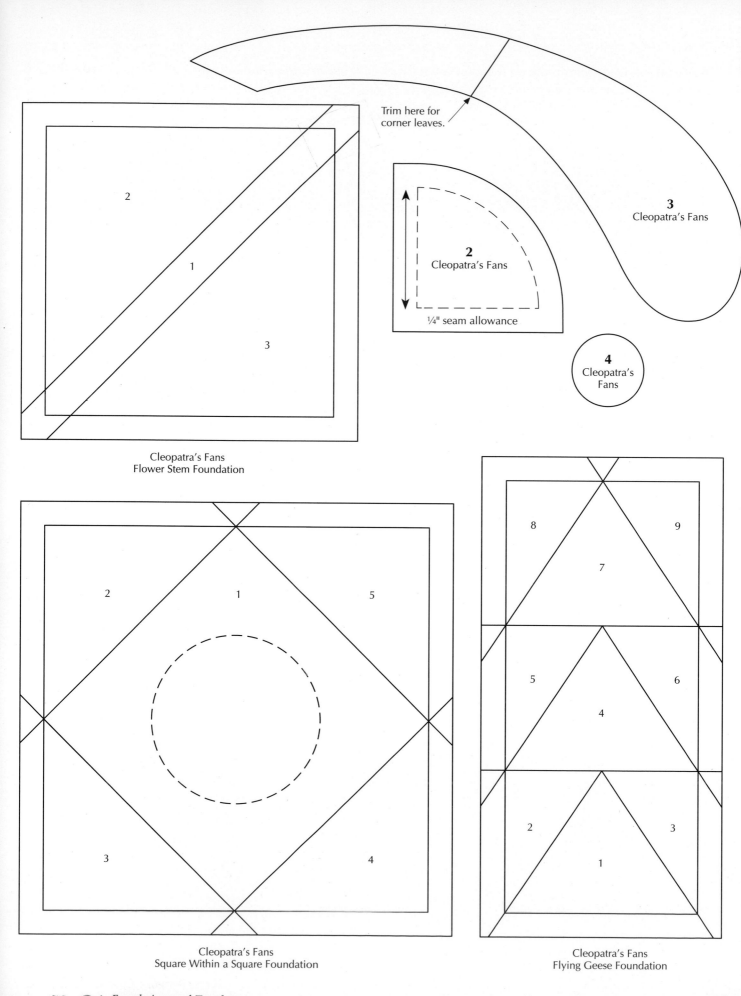

Trim here for corner leaves.

3
Cleopatra's Fans

2
Cleopatra's Fans

¼" seam allowance

4
Cleopatra's
Fans

2

1

3

Cleopatra's Fans
Flower Stem Foundation

2   1   5

3   4

Cleopatra's Fans
Square Within a Square Foundation

8   9

7

5   6

4

2   3

1

Cleopatra's Fans
Flying Geese Foundation

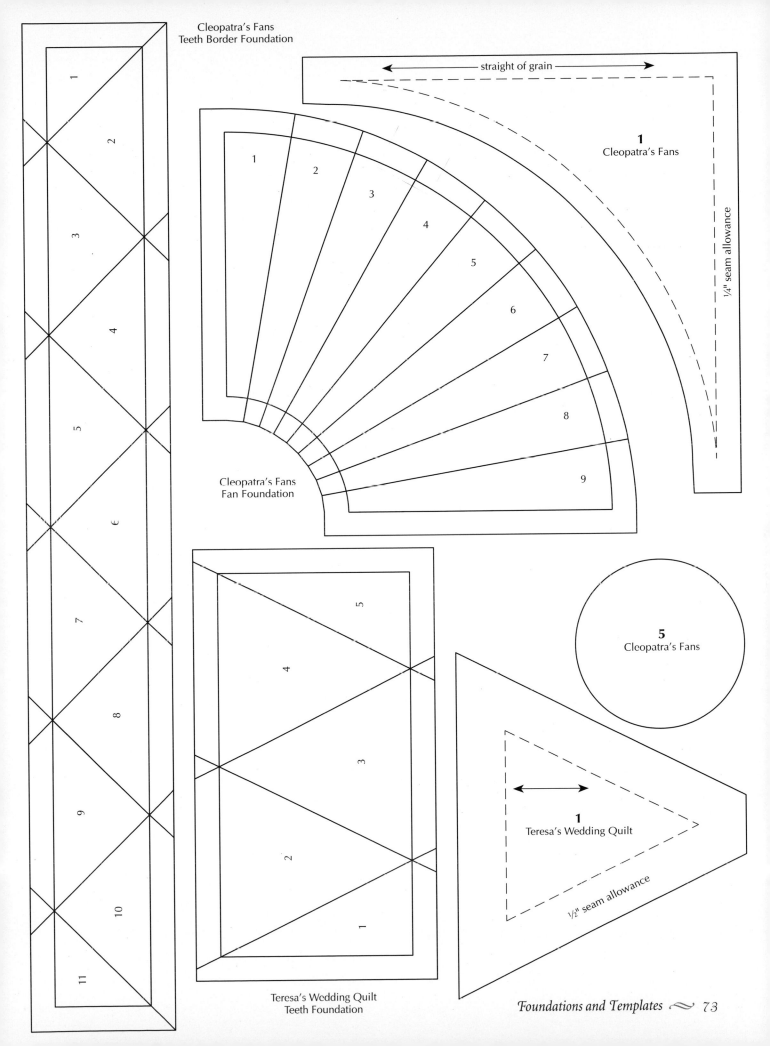

Cleopatra's Fans
Teeth Border Foundation

straight of grain

1
Cleopatra's Fans

¼" seam allowance

Cleopatra's Fans
Fan Foundation

5
Cleopatra's Fans

1
Teresa's Wedding Quilt

½" seam allowance

Teresa's Wedding Quilt
Teeth Foundation

Foundations and Templates ∽ 73

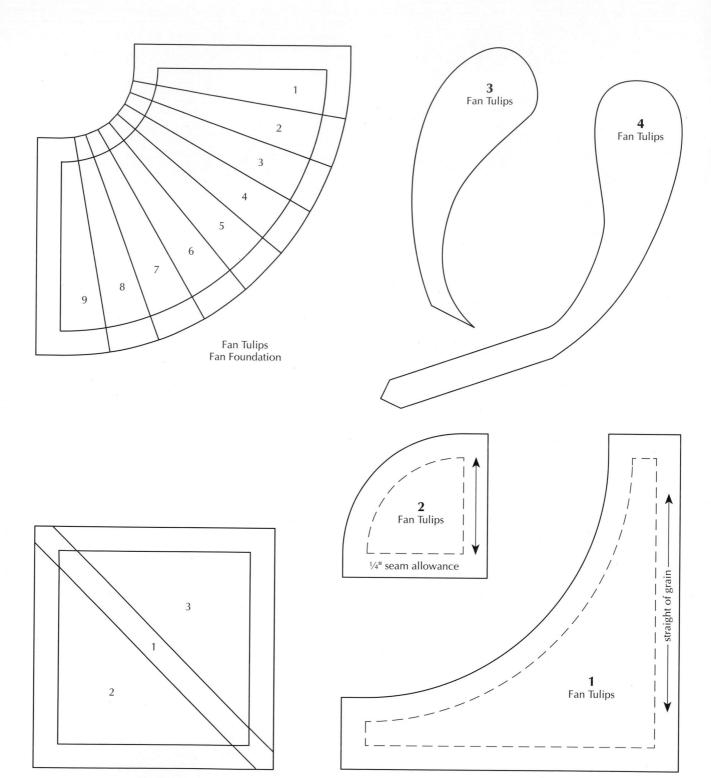

Fan Tulips
Fan Foundation

3
Fan Tulips

4
Fan Tulips

2
Fan Tulips

¼" seam allowance

1
Fan Tulips

straight of grain

Fan Tulips
Flower Stem Foundation

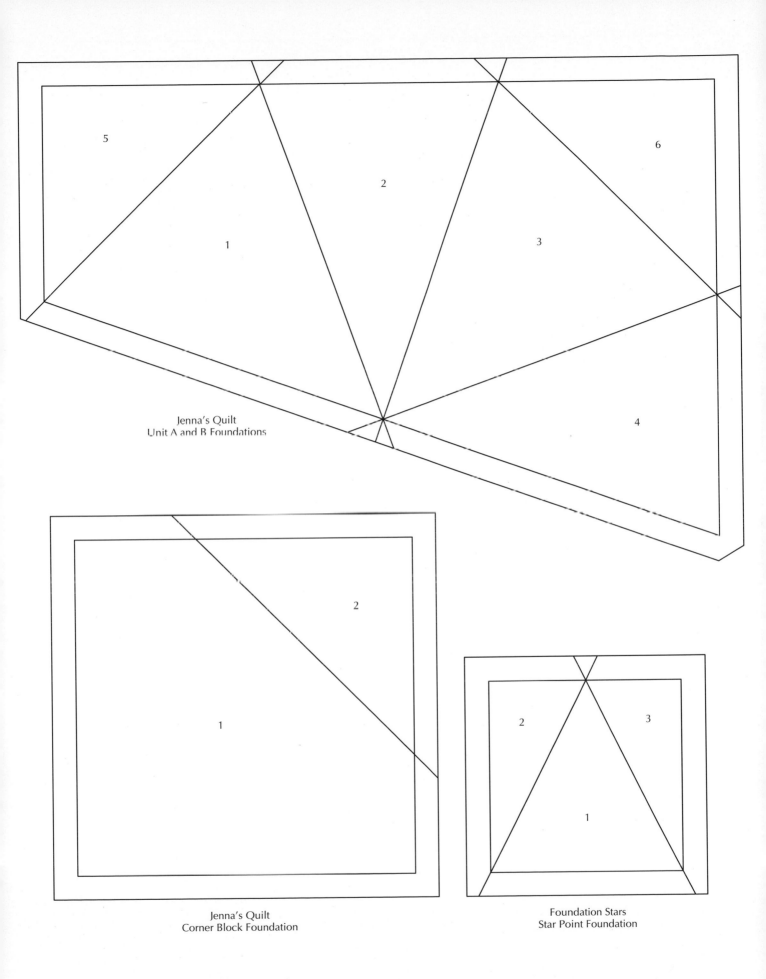

Jenna's Quilt
Unit A and B Foundations

Jenna's Quilt
Corner Block Foundation

Foundation Stars
Star Point Foundation

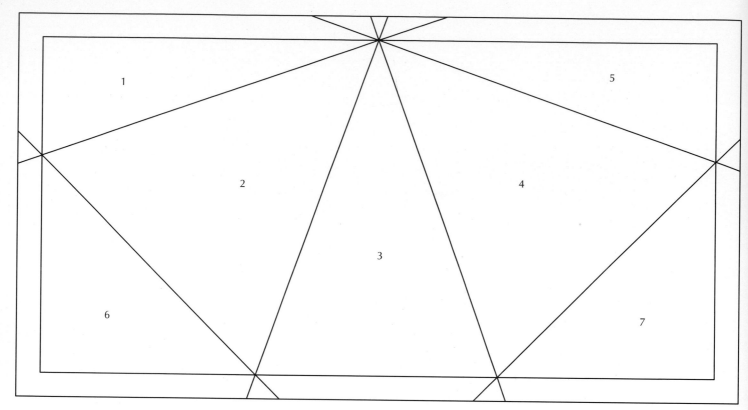

Jenna's Quilt
Unit C Foundation

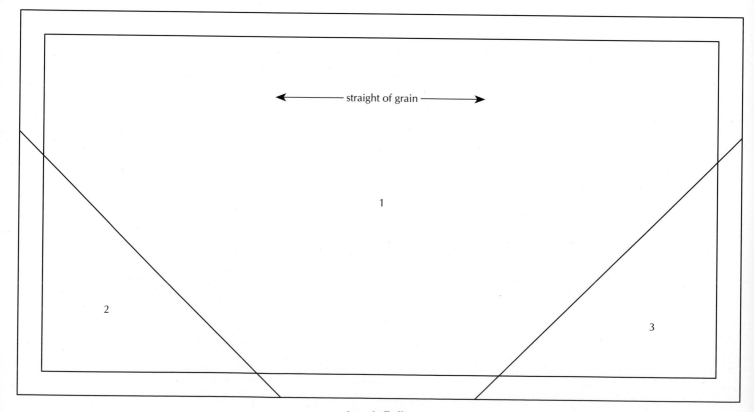

Jenna's Quilt
Unit D Foundation

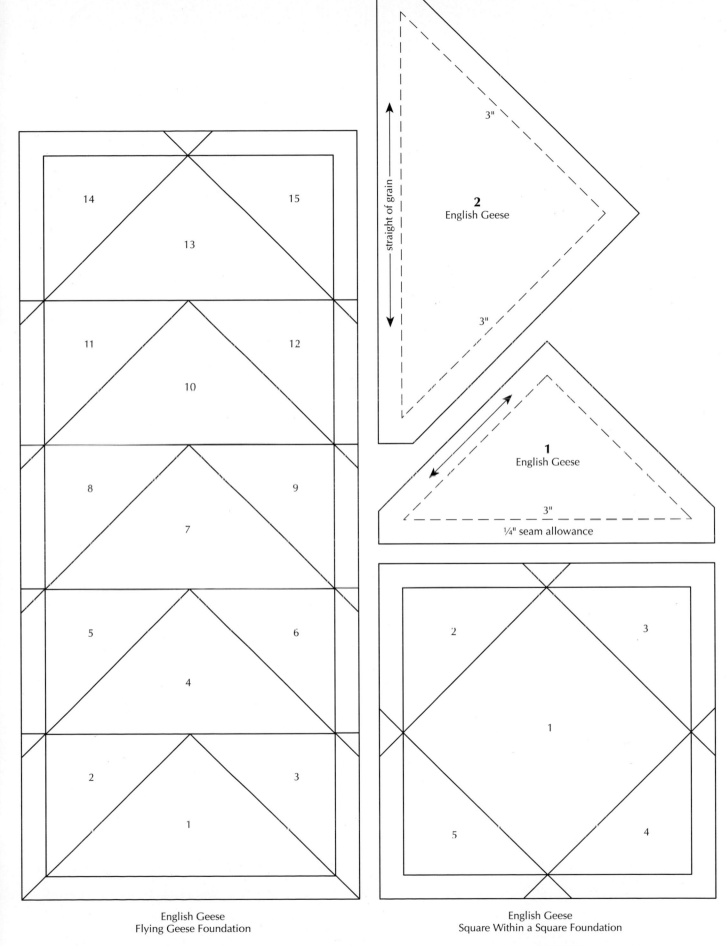

2
English Geese

straight of grain

3"

3"

1
English Geese

3"

¼" seam allowance

14 15

13

11 12

10

8 9

7

5 6

4

2 3

1

2 3

1

5 4

English Geese
Flying Geese Foundation

English Geese
Square Within a Square Foundation

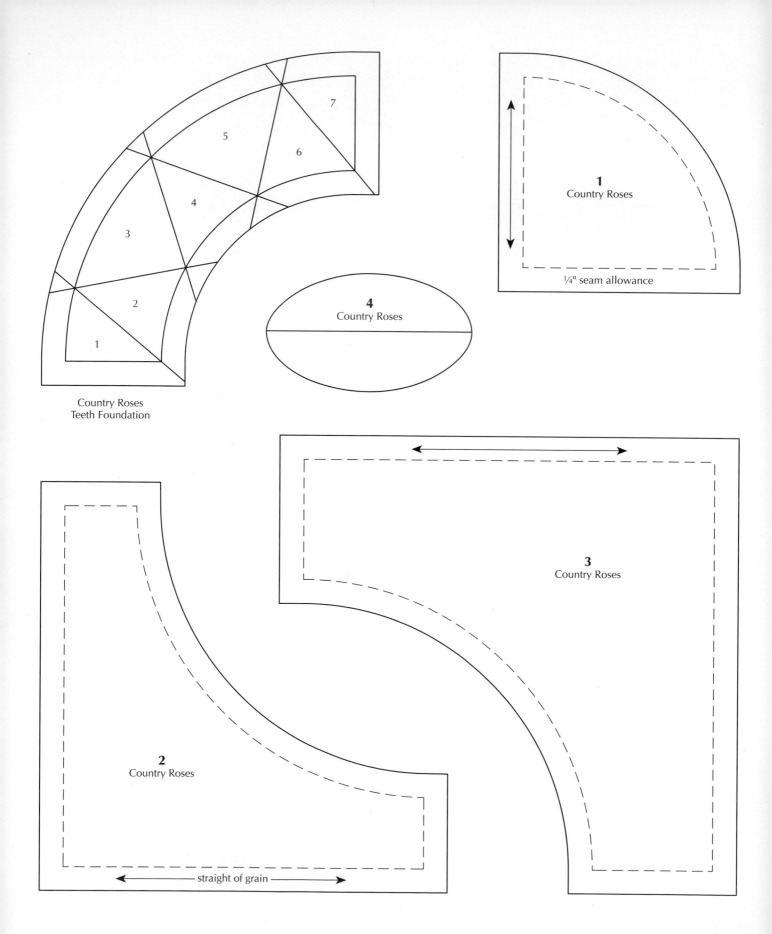

Country Roses
Teeth Foundation

4
Country Roses

1
Country Roses

¼" seam allowance

3
Country Roses

2
Country Roses

← straight of grain →

About the Authors

Tricia Lund remembers being fascinated with her grandmother's quilts as a child, and she always asked to sleep under one when she stayed overnight. This interest was renewed during the Bicentennial quilting revival of the 1970s.

Tricia lives in Seattle with her husband and furry friends. She has a special interest in color and design and their use in traditional scrap quilts. When she's not quilting, she enjoys propagating perennials and roses in her garden, writing long letters to her daughter in the Peace Corps, and doing Master Gardener volunteer work.

Judy Pollard has fond memories of her Aunt Bertha's quilt, a 1930s appliqué design filled with birds, urns, and flowers. Whenever childhood maladies struck, the quilt was hers for the duration to study and choose her favorite combinations of fabric. This early fascination with fabric inspired her to learn to sew (on a treadle machine) and to make her own clothes. In the late 1970s, a quilt store flier led her to a quilting class and a consuming love for quilting. One of her many quilts is a reproduction of Aunt Bertha's.

Judy teaches classes in foundation piecing New York Beauty, Mariner's Compass, and Pickle Dish patterns, among others. She lives in Seattle with her husband and their cat, Smokey.

Publications and Products

THAT PATCHWORK PLACE TITLES:

AMERICA'S BEST-LOVED QUILT BOOKS®

All the Blocks Are Geese • Mary Sue Suit
All New Copy Art for Quilters
All-Star Sampler • Roxanne Carter
Angle Antics • Mary Hickey
Appliqué in Bloom • Gabrielle Swain
Appliquilt® • Tonee White
Appliquilt® for Christmas • Tonee White
Appliquilt® Your ABCs • Tonee White
Around the Block with Judy Hopkins
At Home with Quilts • Nancy J. Martin
Baltimore Bouquets • Mimi Dietrich
Bargello Quilts • Marge Edie
Bias Square® Miniatures • Christine Carlson
Biblical Blocks • Rosemary Makhan
Blockbender Quilts • Margaret J. Miller
Block by Block • Beth Donaldson
Borders by Design • Paulette Peters
Calicoes & Quilts Unlimited
 • Judy Betts Morrison
The Cat's Meow • Janet Kime
Celebrate! with Little Quilts • Alice Berg,
 Sylvia Johnson & Mary Ellen Von Holt
Celebrating the Quilt
Class-Act Quilts
*Classic Quilts with Precise Foundation
 Piecing* • Tricia Lund & Judy Pollard
Colourwash Quilts • Deirdre Amsden
Country Medallion Sampler • Carol Doak
Crazy Rags • Deborah Brunner
Decorate with Quilts & Collections
 • Nancy J. Martin
Down the Rotary Road with Judy Hopkins
The Easy Art of Appliqué
 • Mimi Dietrich & Roxi Eppler
Easy Machine Paper Piecing • Carol Doak
*Easy Mix & Match Machine Paper
 Piecing* • Carol Doak
Easy Paper-Pieced Keepsake Quilts
 • Carol Doak
Easy Reversible Vests • Carol Doak
A Fine Finish • Cody Mazuran
*Five- and Seven-Patch Blocks & Quilts for
 the ScrapSaver* • Judy Hopkins
*Four-Patch Blocks & Quilts for the
 ScrapSaver* • Judy Hopkins
Freedom in Design • Mia Rozmyn
From a Quilter's Garden • Gabrielle Swain
Go Wild with Quilts • Margaret Rolfe
Go Wild with Quilts—Again! • Margaret Rolfe

Great Expectations • Karey Bresenhan
 with Alice Kish & Gay E. McFarland
Hand-Dyed Fabric Made Easy
 • Adriene Buffington
Happy Endings • Mimi Dietrich
Honoring the Seasons • Takako Onoyama
Jacket Jazz • Judy Murrah
Jacket Jazz Encore • Judy Murrah
The Joy of Quilting
 • Joan Hanson & Mary Hickey
Little Quilts • Alice Berg, Sylvia Johnson &
 Mary Ellen Von Holt
Lively Little Logs • Donna McConnell
Loving Stitches • Jeana Kimball
Machine Quilting Made Easy • Maurine Noble
*Magic Base Blocks for Unlimited Quilt
 Designs* • Patty Barney & Cooky Schock
Mirror Manipulations • Gail Valentine
More Jazz from Judy Murrah
*Nine-Patch Blocks & Quilts for the
 ScrapSaver* • Judy Hopkins
Patchwork Pantry
 • Suzette Halferty & Carol C. Porter
A Perfect Match • Donna Lynn Thomas
A Pioneer Doll and Her Quilts • Mary Hickey
*Prairie People—Cloth Dolls to Make and
 Cherish* • Marji Hadley & J. Dianne Ridgley
Press for Success • Myrna Giesbrecht
Quilted for Christmas, Book II
Quilted for Christmas, Book III
Quilted Landscapes • Joan Blalock
Quilted Legends of the West
 • Judy Zehner & Kim Mosher
Quilted Sea Tapestries • Ginny Eckley
Quilting Design Sourcebook • Dorothy Osler
Quilting Makes the Quilt • Lee Cleland
Quilting Up a Storm • Lydia Quigley
Quilts: An American Legacy • Mimi Dietrich
Quilts for Baby • Ursula Reikes
Quilts for Red-Letter Days • Janet Kime
Quilts from the Smithsonian • Mimi Dietrich
Refrigerator Art Quilts • Jennifer Paulson
Repiecing the Past • Sara Rhodes Dillow
Rotary Riot • Judy Hopkins & Nancy J. Martin
Rotary Roundup
 • Judy Hopkins & Nancy J. Martin
Round Robin Quilts
 • Pat Magaret & Donna Slusser
Seasoned with Quilts • Retta Warehime
Sensational Settings • Joan Hanson
*Shortcuts: A Concise Guide to Rotary
 Cutting* • Donna Lynn Thomas
Simply Scrappy Quilts • Nancy J. Martin

Small Talk • Donna Lynn Thomas
Square Dance • Martha Thompson
Start with Squares • Martha Thompson
Strip-Pieced Watercolor Magic
 • Deanna Spingola
Stripples • Donna Lynn Thomas
Sunbonnet Sue All Through the Year
 • Sue Linker
Template-Free® Quiltmaking • Trudie Hughes
Template-Free® Quilts and Borders
 • Trudie Hughes
Through the Window & Beyond
 • Lynne Edwards
Traditional Blocks Meet Appliqué
 • Deborah J. Moffett-Hall
Victorian Elegance • Lezette Thomason
Watercolor Impressions
 • Pat Magaret & Donna Slusser
Watercolor Quilts
 • Pat Magaret & Donna Slusser
Watercolor Quilts 1997 Calendar
 • Pat Magaret & Donna Slusser
Weave It! Quilt It! Wear It!
 • Mary Anne Caplinger
Woven & Quilted • Mary Anne Caplinger
WOW! Wool-on-Wool Folk Art Quilts
 • Janet Carija Brandt

4", 6", 8" & metric Bias Square® • BiRangle™
Ruby Beholder® • ScrapMaster • Rotary Rule™
Rotary Mate™ • Bias Stripper®
Shortcuts to America's Best-Loved Quilts (video)

FIBER STUDIO PRESS TITLES:

FIBER STUDIO PRESS

Complex Cloth • Jane Dunnewold
*Erika Carter: Personal Imagery
 in Art Quilts* • Erika Carter
Inspiration Odyssey • Diana Swim Wessel
The Nature of Design • Joan Colvin
*Velda Newman: A Painter's Approach
 to Quilt Design* • Velda Newman with
 Christine Barnes

Many titles are available at your local quilt shop.
For more information, write for a free color catalog
to That Patchwork Place, Inc., PO Box 118, Bothell,
WA 98041-0118 USA.

☎ U.S. and Canada, call **1-800-426-3126** for the
name and location of the quilt shop nearest you.
Int'l: 1-206-483-3313   **Fax:** 1-206-486-7596
E-mail: info@patchwork.com
Web: www.patchwork.com   11.96